Cem Emrence is a comparative-historical sociologist with interests in state formation, violence, and collective mobilization. His research focuses on the Ottoman Empire and modern Turkey. His new book, *Zones of Rebellion*, is on Kurdish armed contention in contemporary Turkey (Cornell University Press, 2015). His work has appeared in academic journals including the *Journal of Global History*, *Middle East Studies Association Bulletin*, *Middle Eastern Studies*, *Turkish Studies* and *Comparative Sociology*.

'In *Remapping the Middle East*, Cem Emrence analyzes the paradigms in which late Ottoman history has been written. His original contribution is the conceptualisation of the body of work produced in recent decades on social and cultural history, and the analysis of the latter's linkages to the earlier currents of modernisation and dependency studies. Emrence approaches the relatively new trend under the rubric of bargaining perspectives, repositions its relationship to the centre and 'macro' trends, but goes beyond binary constructs such as centre-periphery and state-society by investigating multi-faceted networks on the regional and imperial level. The combination of synthetic and analytical skills Emrence displays in his work is remarkable. He has internalised a vast body of historical literature, which he skilfully and creatively distils through the lens of social scientific concepts and categories. The result is a significant contribution to late Ottoman Studies.'

Hasan Kayalı, Associate Professor of History, University of California

'Cem Emrence has an excellent mastery of the historical and theoretical literature, and an elegant and genuinely novel model of the social transformation of imperial populations. He argues that there were parallel but divergent forces in the different geographies of the Ottoman Empire, impelling different forms of negotiation both with the centre and with European imposition. This book is an important contribution to the growing field of the historical sociology of empires and a milestone in Ottoman Studies.'

Çağlar Keyder, Professor of Sociology, Binghamton University, SUNY

REMAPPING THE OTTOMAN MIDDLE EAST

Modernity, Imperial Bureaucracy and Islam

CEM EMRENCE

I.B. TAURIS
LONDON · NEW YORK

Paperback edition published in 2016 by
I.B.Tauris & Co. Ltd
London • New York
www.ibtauris.com

Copyright © 2012 Cem Emrence

The right of Cem Emrence to be identified as the author of this work has been asserted by the author in accordance with the Copyright, Designs and Patent Act 1988.

All rights reserved. Except for brief quotations in a review, this book, or any part thereof, may not be reproduced, stored in or introduced into a retrieval system, or transmitted, in any form or by any means, electronic, mechanical, photocopying, recording or otherwise, without the prior written permission of the publisher.

ISBN: 978 1 78453 161 4
eISBN: 978 0 85772 999 6

A full CIP record for this book is available from the British Library
A full CIP record for this book is available from the Library of Congress

Library of Congress catalog card: available

Typeset by Newgen Publishers, Chennai
Printed and bound by CPI Group (UK) Ltd, Croydon, CR0 4YY

CONTENTS

List of Illustrations vii
Acknowledgements xi
Note on Transliteration xiii

Introduction 1
   Method 2
   Imperial Paths 4
   Theory 8
   Background and Plan of the Book 10

1 **Historiography** 15
   Modernization Approaches 17
   Macro Models 21
   Bargaining Perspectives 27
   Conclusions 32

2 **Coast** 35
   The Making of a Globally-Connected Economy 36
   Middle Class Hegemony 41
   Economic Contention 46
   Conclusions 50

3 **Interior** 55
   An Urban Muslim Bloc 55

Creating Regional Markets	62
Patrimonial Tensions	67
Conclusions	74
4 Frontier	**75**
Politics of Emergency	76
Collecting Protection Money	84
Rebellious Repertoires	90
Conclusions	97
5 Routes of Transformation, 1908–1922	**101**
The New Imperial Class	102
Nationalizing the Coast	107
Failed Bargains in the Interior	110
Making Frontiers Independent	115
Conclusions	119
Conclusion	**121**
Late Ottoman Trajectories	121
Ottoman Insights	124
A New Research Agenda	128
Notes	131
Bibliography	155
Index	185

ILLUSTRATIONS

Illustrations

Military strengthening. The First Battalion of the First
Infantry Regiment of the Imperial Guard. (Abdulhamid II
Collection, Library of Congress, LC-USZ62-38077) 19

Economic independence. Removing the French post
box in Jerusalem with the abrogation of capitulations.
(American Colony (Jerusalem), Library of Congress,
LC-DIG-ppmsca-13709-00243) 26

Bargaining with locals. Ali Ekrem Bey in
Beersheba, 1905. (American Colony (Jerusalem),
Library of Congress, LC-DIG-ppmsca-13709-00134) 29

Rise of regional port towns. The construction
of Haifa Railroad. 40

Symbol of modernity. Clock Tower of Izmir. 44

Cosmopolitanism. Galata Bridge connecting the old
and the new in Istanbul. (Library of Congress,
LC-DIG-ppmsca-03801) 45

Trade in a multi-cultural setting. A Christian
merchant from Aydın, a rabbi from Izmir, and a
Muslim merchant from Manisa, 1873. (Les costumes
populaires de la Turquie en 1873, Library of Congress,
LC-USZC4-11714) 47

Connected to global flows. Pera neighboorhood in
Istanbul. (Abdulhamid II Collection, Library of Congress,
LC-USZ62-81654) 51

Eliminating the rural hero. Bedouin. (American Colony
(Jerusalem), Library of Congress, LC-DIG-ppmsca-13195) 58

Training the imperial bureaucrat. Imperial School
of Civil Service students (Mekteb-i Mülkiye-i Şahane).
(Abdulhamid II Collection, Library of Congress,
LC-USZ62-81997) 61

Training the imperial bureaucrat. Law School
Building. (Abdulhamid II Collection, Library of Congress,
LC-USZ62-81994) 61

Istanbul style. An upscale Damascus home at the turn of the
century. (University of Pennslyvania Museum,
DD2000–00530) 62

The new Arab-Imperial elite. Maktab Anbar in
Damascus after renovation. Aga Khan Trust for Culture. 70

The new Arab-Imperial elite. Students from
imperial middle school in Aleppo. (Abdulhamid II
Collection, LC-USZ62-80856) 71

Extending the imperial reach. Opening of Hijaz Railway. 77

'Taming' the Ottoman frontiers. Tribal School
(Aşiret Mektebi) students in Istanbul. (Abdulhamid II
Collection, Library of Congress, LC-USZ62-81454) 79

'Taming' the Ottoman frontiers. Tribal School
(Aşiret Mektebi) students in Istanbul. (Abdulhamid II
Collection, Library of Congress, LC-USZ62-81469) 80

Inventing traditions. Ali Ekrem Bey presenting robes of
honor in Beersheba. (American Colony (Jerusalem), Library of
Congress, LC-DIG-ppmsca-13709-00134) 82

Protection sellers. A member of Harb tribe (of Medina)
with a rifle. (Les costumes populaires de la
Turquie en 1873, Library of Congress, LC-USZC4-11727) 88

ILLUSTRATIONS IX

The new imperial class and positivism. Medical School (Tıbbiye Mektebi) students. (Abdulhamid II Collection, Library of Congress, LC-USZ62-82006)	103
Projecting an Ottoman identity. Religious leaders and imperial elite at the ballot-box.	105
War mobilization. Recruiting for the army near Tiberias, 1914. (American Colony (Jerusalem), Library of Congress, LC-DIG-ppmsca-13709-00009)	113
Ottoman army. Ottoman soldiers' daily ration in Palestine, 1917. (American Colony (Jerusalem), Library of Congress, LC-DIG-ppmsca-13709-00167)	113
Call for Jihad. Sharif of Medina supporting the Ottoman war effort in Medina, 1914. (American Colony (Jerusalem), Library of Congress, LC-DIG-ppmsca-13709-00005)	117

Figures

1	Three Waves of Late Ottoman Historiography	16
2	Collective Action in the Ottoman Frontier	96

ACKNOWLEDGEMENTS

Several people helped me to turn an ambitious research agenda into a book. I would like to thank the editors of the *Journal of Global History and Middle East Studies Association Bulletin* who allowed me to discuss my ideas about Ottoman historiography in their journals. A concise version of the argument here first appeared in 'Imperial Paths, Big Comparisons: The Late Ottoman Empire', *Journal of Global History*, Vol. 3 (3), 2008, 289–311, and an earlier version of Chapter 1 first appeared in 'Three Waves of Late Ottoman Historiography, 1950–2007', *Middle East Studies Association Bulletin*, Vol. 41 (2), 2007, 137–151. Participants of the Great Lakes Ottoman Workshop at the University of Michigan (2007) shared with me their knowledge of the Ottoman frontiers. A presentation at the Contentious Politics Workshop at Columbia University (2007) was instrumental to locate the intellectual boundaries of the project. A pre-organized panel about comparative empires at the Annual Meeting of American Historical Association (2009) proved to be useful to rethink the Ottomans from a comparative perspective. My dissertation committee at Binghamton University raised important conceptual and methodological questions which I later addressed in the book. The comments of my advisor, Çağlar Keyder, were especially helpful. I made the final touches in the book at the University of

Massachusetts-Amherst where I am a post-doctoral fellow in the department of history.

I would also like to use this opportunity to thank Şevket Pamuk who supported my professional development throughout the years. Hasan Kayalı not only read the manuscript in its entirety but also was always there when I needed help regarding my professional career. My editors at I.B.Tauris, Joanna Godfrey, Jenna Steventon, and Tomasz Hoskins have been supportive and provided feedback. Daniel Chard helped me with the copyediting issues. My family also deserves a big thank you note as they endured the graduate school and the writing process of this book. Finally, Ayşegül has been with me throughout these difficult but happy years.

NOTE ON TRANSLITERATION

I have used the modern Turkish spelling for terms and names throughout the text.

INTRODUCTION

With the end of the cold war, the Balkans and the Middle East have hit the headlines on a daily basis. Both regions have turned into major conflict zones where state sovereignty and collective identity are redefined in important ways. For the distant observer, failed states, communal violence and resistance to the West provided the much needed mental map to locate the human tragedies from Bosnia to Iraq. In this view, political conflict in Eurasia is a natural outcome of historical tensions between ethno–religious and civilizational units. Lending support to this argument, empire historian Anthony Pagden recently suggested that the region has been the battleground between East and West for centuries.[1]

Commonsense views reflect a fundamental claim about the region's history: that the Eurasian experience is characterized by antagonistic cultural identities that are mobilized by great-power competition and hostile nation-states throughout history. Acting as intellectual derivatives, the clash-of-civilizations arguments, confessional wars, the discourse of Balkanization, cold-war rivalries and nationalist imagery are deployed to make sense of the past and explain the present to contemporary audiences. A major deficit in this comprehensive and yet simplistic account is that it misses the Ottoman input in the region's transition to modernity during the nineteenth century.

The scholarship on the Ottoman Empire has not addressed the issue either. Late Ottoman Studies approach the imperial experience in terms of the modernizing vision of the state elites, the decisive impact of the world economy, or the resilient nature of local dynamics. Meanwhile, the more popular nation-state accounts view the late Ottoman period from a nationalist angle, portraying an unjust and/or ineffective Ottoman state. Despite their differences, both literatures have one thing in common: they fail to deliver imperial accounts that reveal the multiple transitions of late Ottoman societies to the modern world.

This book aims to accomplish that task and unveil alternative paths to modernity in the Ottoman Middle East. For this purpose, it presents an intra-empire perspective and explains the variation in the Ottoman world with reference to historical trajectories. Disagreeing with linear and state-centric models of history, I argue in this book that the coast, the interior and the frontier emerged as distinct imperial paths during the nineteenth century. Each Ottoman path represented a unique order in the region and produced important outcomes for the modern Middle East.

Method

I employ the concept of historical trajectory to understand the variation in the Ottoman world. The trajectory approach suggests that the historical experience is spatially-diverse, temporally-bounded, and follows a path-dependent pattern. Path-dependency comes into effect when key decisions made at junction points persist over time and produce long-term outcomes.[2] Accordingly, this research agenda investigates the locked-in effects of state–society and global–local relations that have become entrenched over time because of high reversal costs. High reversal costs stem from set-up expenditures or increasing returns over time. While the former reveals the bounding character of initial decisions, the latter demonstrates the benefits accrued with successful learning processes.[3]

Trajectory analysis views causality in history from a path-dependent perspective. It specifies eventful origins, underlines reinforcing processes, and looks for important outcomes. As Andrew Abbott points out, turning points represent abrupt and chaotic moments that open up the possibility for networks to rearrange.[4] While the subsequent episode strengthens the new direction, it is the processes that turn episodes into stable trajectories. Key processes do this by acting as positive feedback mechanisms. As Kathleen Thelen noted sometime ago, stability cannot be taken for granted; it is something that has to be sustained.[5]

Path-dependency ideas inspired innovative research. Examining state-building in early modern Europe, Thomas Ertman showed that it was the timing of geopolitical competition and the organization of the local government that paved the way for distinct political regimes in the region.[6] James Mahoney demonstrated how the choices of domestic elites at a junction point vis-à-vis the question of state-building and commercialization of agriculture consolidated different political regimes in Central America.[7] Examining post-socialist transformations in Eastern Europe, David Stark and Laszlo Bruszt concluded that regional divergence is the outcome of different institutional choices regarding privatization and citizenship rights.[8]

The analytical strength of path-dependency approach then lies in its ability to explain patterned diversity in a universe. Contemporary scholarship has documented alternative routes to state formation in Latin America, regional origins of fascism in interwar Italy, and the evolution of distinct welfare regimes in Europe.[9] In this vein, the path-dependency approach departed from convergence accounts and systemic narratives in social sciences that respectively assume the existence of a singular path (i.e. modernization) or explain social change in terms of a single variable (i.e. capitalism).[10] It is also different from continuity arguments in the history field, that offer a static analysis of durable structures or deep-rooted ideologies.

Shifting the focus from turning points to path-making processes themselves, this project suggests that it was local politics, economy and contention that shaped the Ottoman Middle East during the nineteenth century. First, they were key sites to accumulate power, wealth and status in late Ottoman society. Second, their interactive character consolidated the power of interlocked leaderships.[11] Third, the three processes in turn shaped local hierarchies, defined the specific bargains between 'peripheries' and the Ottoman state, and determined the nature of interactions between imperial agents and global society.

Following these guidelines, my arguments in this study will be three-fold. First, economy on the coast, politics in the interior, and contention in the frontier served as primary processes that initiated regional paths in the late Ottoman Empire. Second, Ottoman trajectories were consolidated when there was convergence among economic, political and contention forms, yet these processes institutionalized differently in each path. Finally, the Ottoman paths were also the making of regional actors that utilized global capitalism, state transformation, and geopolitical competition to build competing imperial experiences. Overall, the book suggests that understanding the nineteenth century Ottoman world and its legacy should start from exploring the regionally-constituted, network-based and path-dependent historical trajectories.

Imperial Paths

The Ottoman Middle East was characterized by three historical trajectories during the nineteenth century. These were the coast, the interior and the frontier. The coastal framework represented the port-cities and commercial hinterlands of western Anatolia and the eastern Mediterranean littoral; the interior path marked the inland experience of Anatolia, Syria and Palestine; and the frontier incorporated the contentious borderland regions of eastern Anatolia, Iraq and the Arabian Peninsula. In a snapshot, the

Ottoman trajectories were shaped by market relations and the discourse of modernity on the coast, the imperial bureaucracy and the notion of Islamic state in the interior, and religious trust networks and politics of mobilization in the frontier.

The coastal path was initiated by the world economy. Built after foreign trade, the coastal model carved out a new economic geography which benefited the domestic non-Muslim merchants the most and paved the way for middle-class hegemony in major port-cities.[12] The new historical setting was also a consequence of the expanding public sphere and found its expression in reformist port-city press, autonomous municipal councils, and class-coalitional politics. Towards the end of the century, merchants and professionals implemented middle-class rule on the Ottoman coast and shaped the coastal space around the values of cosmopolitanism, free trade and modernity.

The inland regions merged into a single historical trajectory between 1840 and 1860. A window of opportunity was opened in Syria and Palestine after the withdrawal of Egyptian forces in 1841. After two decades of crisis, the Muslim bloc pre-mpted the rise of non-Muslim merchant classes, and Ottoman centralization measures blocked the path to further autonomous rule. Subsequently, the imperial center sealed a new political contract with the urban Muslim bloc, reproducing the familial coalitions in the interior. Bureaucratic governance attached economic opportunities to political power, sustained the ideological hegemony of Sunni Islam, and shaped contention towards patrimonial conflicts around the Ottoman state.[13]

The Ottoman frontier was set on a new track during the age of imperialism. Representing the largest collective action effort in the Middle East, political mobilization was rural in nature, operated through religious brokerage, and perceived the imperial state as a corrupt and immoral entity.[14] Directing communal resistance against the central state, frontiers had a better chance of institutionalizing local autonomy. This was especially the case when the local elite possessed moral authority, kept its power-base outside bureaucratic structures, and secured economic survival through protection rents. Furthermore, imperial rivalries granted an extra-space to frontier leaderships for deal-making with Ottomans and third parties at the same time.[15]

Political coalitions, economic networks, and collective claims sustained the distinct character of Ottoman trajectories. It was the middle classes on the coast, urban Muslim coalitions in the interior, and religious trust networks in the frontier that governed the region. While municipal and administrative councils tied the first two to the public politics of the empire, the frontier leaderships operated in and out of the state. Economic forms were also trajectory-specific. Non-Muslim merchants traded cash crops for the world market on the coast whereas it was large landholding and regional markets that consolidated the power of Muslim interests in the interior.[16] Frontier leaderships were able to oppose both types of commercialization and collected protection rents for economic and political survival.

Contentious collective action had a unique repertoire in each Ottoman trajectory. In the coastal path, port-city mobilizations were the outcome of distributional conflicts which were fought over new economic riches. In the interior, elite Muslim households competed for precious bureaucratic posts once artisan discontent and non-Muslim challengers disappeared from the scene. In the frontiers, religious entrepreneurs forged communal protest identities to organize large-scale movements. In sum, it was market-based contention, patrimonial politics, and discourses of autonomy and religious revival that operated as the ideological and material bases of claim-making in the Ottoman Middle East.

The late Ottoman Empire was characterized by socially and materially distinct political geographies during the nineteenth century. *Thin rule* defined the arid frontiers where rural–religious networks operating on protection rents clashed with the Ottoman state over centralization. There was *contested rule* on the coast where non-Muslim middle classes enjoyed the spoils of foreign trade and European services but had limited political bargains with the Ottoman state. *Consensual rule* characterized the interior experience where the unrivalled hegemony of the late Ottoman state was backed up by bureaucratic institutions, domestic markets, and a powerful Sunni bloc.[17]

Ottoman trajectories produced long-term outcomes. The coast became the spatial seat of modernity, embodying middle-class values, global interactions, and a broad public sphere. State-led transformation and conservative values dominated the inland regions where legitimacy of the state and moral values of Sunni Islam characterized the interior. Geopolitical competition blocked the path to successful state-building in the frontiers, allowing the local interests to bargain effectively with the central state for autonomy. Despite the political intervention of nation-state framework later in the twentieth century, the coast preserved its global outlook; the interior kept its conservative identity; and the frontiers utilized insurgency and heterodox Islam to make political statements.

It would be helpful at this point to clarify the central concepts used in this study. The broadest analytical claim made in the book is that each Ottoman trajectory represented a distinct path to modernity in the Middle East. I define modernity as an episode of world order that was characterized by capitalist expansion, fast-track state-building, and imperialist competition at the turn of the twentieth century. What I mean by historical trajectory then is an articulation with a key aspect of the modernist project by developing routine relations between local, imperial and global actors. Accordingly, this study views historical trajectory as a temporally and spatially bounded social formation that represents a distinct (economic, political and moral) order with a path-dependent character.

Late Ottoman trajectories had common properties. First, each path utilized economic and political resources as well as cultural frames to carve out a regional order. Second, path-making was an active process rather than a pre-given historical reality. A mere location on the coastline, inland region or a border zone did not necessarily mean 'free admission' to a historical trajectory. Third, the strength of any historical path in a specific location depended on the degree of compatibility among key processes. Fourth, Ottoman paths emerged in a sequential order that tried to contain (coast–interior) or replicate (interior–frontier) the experience of the antecedent path. Finally, Ottoman trajectories were uneven formations distributing resources and leadership in an unequal fashion. It was major port-cities, provincial inland capitals, and far frontiers that benefited the most from each Ottoman path.

I also argue in the following pages that the late Ottoman trajectories enjoyed competing social bases. The middle classes of the coast refer to domestic merchants and professional groups who were connected to global flows and operated as vanguards of modernization in the eastern Mediterranean world. The Urban Muslim Bloc was a composite leadership who established a hegemonic presence in inland regions by controlling land, local bureaucracy, and moral order in late Ottoman society. Following Charles Tilly, I define frontier societies as trust networks who successfully limited the access of outsiders to community resources.[18] Frontier leaderships functioned as gatekeepers in Ottoman society and mobilized distinct cultural frames (such as religious messages) to protect communal and/or regional autonomy.

Theory

This study has eclectic theoretical origins despite its strong intellectual ties to historical institutionalism. I have benefited from a variety of schools in history and social sciences to explain each Ottoman path throughout the book. World-systems analysis and new economic sociology showed how the coastal trajectory came into being with global economic incorporation and later was transformed into a novel middle-class setting with the input of domestic actors. The key was the locally-embedded character of the economy. It is no wonder that circuits of commerce relied on trust, reciprocity and cultural conventions, and economic outcomes largely depended upon effective control over communication lines and information flows on the Ottoman coast.[19]

I have used the institutionalist explanation to understand the durable nature of Ottoman rule in the interior. The Ottoman institutions solved the collective-action problems of the Muslim bloc by coordinating elite interests, generating common cultural scripts around Sunni Islam, and providing social mobility to Muslim citizens. Compliance to Ottoman rule was based on what Margaret Levi calls "credible commitments and fair procedures."[20] The Ottoman world was predictable; the state honored its commitments; and no social actors appeared on the interior scene with rival cultural schemas and economic resources. As Arthur Stinchcombe reminds us, institutions can only function well with the perfect combination of resources and believable commitment.[21]

Basic insights from rational-choice institutionalism and contentious-politics literature proved extremely useful to explain thin rule in the frontiers. As rational-choice analysts argue persuasively, principal–agent problems limit the power of the central state in outlying areas because of high monitoring costs, and weak state presence enables the locals to use rebellion as a bargaining strategy.[22] If mass mobilization is an effective way to strike deals with the center, contentious-politics literature showed how it was done in the Ottoman frontiers. Acting as powerful movement brokers, religious entrepreneurs relied on pre-existing tribal ties, mobilized heterodox brands of Islam, and utilized the expanding political opportunity space to protect local autonomy.[23]

The economic bases of autonomy in the frontier became clear for me with the help of institutional economics. The absence of state as an enforcer of contracts was an important reason as to why the Ottoman frontiers did not experience market integration to the same degree as compared to the rest of the empire.[24] Still, as Roy Bin Wong argued for Qing China, informal mechanisms can be as important as formal rules in economic exchange.[25] With this idea in mind, I have discussed various informal constraints on markets such as protection rents and religious fees that not only blocked market integration in Middle Eastern frontiers, but also served the economic well-being of frontier leaderships.

The trajectory model proposed in the book also benefited from spatial approaches in the world-history field. The spatial model called for new units of analysis in writing imperial histories by demonstrating the fact that empires were not homogenous entities. The recent monographs on Russian and Chinese frontiers, as well as burgeoning research on seas and littoral zones, have equally made it clear that coasts and frontiers accumulated distinct (imperial) experiences.[26] Taking a similar direction, this study promotes a trajectory-specific account of late Ottoman history, departing from top-down imperial histories, retrospective nationalist narratives, and micro history studies.

The spatial turn that this study takes needs to be qualified in order to separate it from purely geographical perspectives. Thomas Gieryn warns us that it is only places (not spaces) that give durability to social identities, cultural norms and economic hierarchies.[27] It is not mere geography but rather its institutional properties and organizational structuring that shape the experience of a specific location.[28] In that respect, geography operated as a necessary but not a sufficient condition for the emergence of Ottoman paths. Late Ottoman territories experienced distinct types of place-making because of capitalism, state centralization and inter-state competition which in turn produced the coast, interior and frontier as regional trajectories during the nineteenth century.

Background and Plan of the Book

This project is built upon the interplay of ideas and evidence. While world-systems research, the world-history field, network analysis, the institutional school, historical sociology, contentious-politics literature and debates on social-science methodology certainly improved the final product, it is to my fellow historians of the Ottoman Empire whom I owe a great deal. This study could not have been undertaken without the important steps taken in the field that produced three impressive bodies of knowledge in the last thirty years. These have been the growth in the political-economy literature on the Ottoman Empire during the 1980s, the Arab historiography on the Ottoman Middle East during the 1990s, and the more recent critical accounts of the late Ottoman past regarding the frontiers and marginal groups.

Contemporary realities also shaped the way I think about the Ottomans. The end of the cold war, the demise of the nation-state order, and changing forms of legitimacy and identity in the Middle East have finally brought the "imperial moment" back that kept its traumas and failures but also successes hidden in the box for a long time. The common ground has suddenly become obvious: to revise the Western impact and give more authorship to the Ottoman state and the local actors in the making of the region. It is this message that the book wants to take further. As such, my intention is neither an unqualified eulogy to the empire nor an outright condemnation of the late Ottoman past. The idea is to make a critical assessment of the imperial past by tracing the diverse record of the Ottomans in different regions.[29]

The limitations of this work should also be made clear from the outset. My analysis of the Ottoman Empire leaves the Balkans and North Africa outside the borders of this study. This is done for analytical reasons. I believe that "the other historical routes" to the late Ottoman Empire require different causal dynamics and large-scale processes to examine in the first place. Colonialism and white-settlers in North Africa, and nationalism and great power intervention in the Balkans were just two points that have to be factored in to the analysis. Likewise, despite its cursory treatment in the book, eastern Anatolia, Macedonia, and Kosovo need to be evaluated as part of a distinct historical path where there was nationalist agitation, inter-communal violence, and geopolitical rivalry after the Berlin Congress (1878). Thus, I leave the study of other Ottoman paths (colonial, nationalist and conflict) to another volume.

On intellectual terms, this is an analytically-driven historical study to incorporate the Ottoman case to larger debates in comparative historical social science and world history. It uses a causal-narrative structure and a relational macro-historical approach to chart long-term historical patterns and trace important outcomes. Hence, it gives more weight to medium-range theory building, conceptual framework and methodological concerns. Unlike the conventional research routine on the Ottoman Empire, then, this study surveys all Asian provinces of the Ottoman Empire for more than a hundred years in order to capture patterned diversity within the imperial universe.

Accordingly, I have not examined primary sources about a specific location or a time frame that are available in imperial, national, regional and colonial archives. Instead, I utilized most of the available and expanding literatures on the late Ottoman Empire and complemented that with a wide range of readings from social sciences and history. The latter included theoretical readings from political science and sociology, methodological debates from social sciences, and comparative cases from world history and historical sociology. The synthetic approach allowed me to construct the late Ottoman experience around a theoretically-guided agenda and come up with an empirically reliable comparative analysis.

On the whole, the book provides fresh answers to a variety of important questions regarding the late Ottoman past in the Middle East. To mention a few, what was the nature of late Ottoman rule that secured ideological legitimacy and yet could not prevent imperial collapse? How did Islam legitimize the Ottoman state and yet function as a protest ideology? What did cosmopolitanism, autonomy and frontier politics mean in the Middle East? Is it meaningful to discuss civil society in the Ottoman Empire? What was new about the Ottoman experience during the nineteenth century? Can a regional-trajectory approach help us see Young Turks era and Arab nationalism under a different light? Finally, what were the key Ottoman legacies that shaped the region during the twentieth century? [30]

The book tries to answer these critical questions in five chapters. Chapter 1 provides a detailed discussion on late Ottoman historiography and concludes that the field operates with dualistic accounts and state-centered narratives. The remaining chapters introduce a trajectory perspective. Chapter 2 traces the creation of middle-class settings in the eastern Mediterranean littoral. Chapter 3 demonstrates the power of Muslim coalitions in central Anatolia, Syria and Palestine. Focusing on eastern Anatolia, Iraq, and the Arabian Peninsula, Chapter 4 answers the key question of why the Ottomans had thin rule in the frontiers. Chapter 5 unveils the resilient character of regional trajectories in the closing years of the empire and demonstrates that mass politics and major wars revised the Ottoman paths, yet did not destroy them.

CHAPTER 1

HISTORIOGRAPHY

There have been three waves of late Ottoman historiography since the second half of the twentieth century. Each rose to prominence in a different global context, maintained almost complete hegemony for two decades, and was later replaced by an upcoming intellectual current. Changing historical approaches also meant that the field of Ottoman Studies enjoyed distinct thematic choices, frameworks and methodologies which were in line with worldwide trends in historiography.[1] It will be my argument here that the three episodes of late Ottoman history writing can be classified as modernization approaches, macro models and bargaining perspectives.

Modernization approaches were extremely influential in understanding top-down political change in the late Ottoman context. They set the tone for and confirmed the pre-eminent position of political, intellectual and diplomatic history in Ottoman Studies. Focusing on world economy, macro models pushed the Ottoman Studies towards dependency and world-systems perspectives and introduced social and economic history to the field. Bargaining perspectives have unseated modernization and global capitalism as the key variables in understanding the late Ottoman Empire. Inspired by institutionalism, postcolonial analysis, and microhistory studies, the new scholarship turned the attention to state and society relations and promoted a negotiation model to explain the Ottoman past.

This chapter reviews the historiographical trends in late Ottoman Studies by a comparative discussion. I will do this by unpacking each wave around the same analytical questions. My analysis will demonstrate that the Ottoman scholarship associated with each wave has a different idea when it comes to locating the macro-historical dynamic, identifying the turning point, registering the main process, and projecting the ultimate direction in Ottoman history. As a helpful short cut, Figure 1 summarizes the evolution of late Ottoman historiography, the main arguments of each wave, and the major differences among them.

Four caveats are in order for the discussion below. First, I do not evaluate each wave on a purely theoretical basis but rather focus on its reflection in late Ottoman Studies. Second, my analysis favors the common ground in each wave that is neither all-inclusive nor oriented towards a single study. Third, the fact that each wave is considered to be hegemonic in a certain time frame does not necessarily mean that studies of the same genre stopped appearing afterwards or lost credibility in a dramatic fashion. Finally, there have always been synthetic works that combine a variety of waves, approaches and agendas of late Ottoman history writing.[2]

	Modernization Approaches, 1950–70	Macro Models, 1970–90	Bargaining Perspectives, 1990–
Causal Dynamic	West	World Economy	Imperial Consolidation
Turning Point	Tanzimat	Intro. of Foreign Trade	Centralization
Main Process	Westernization	Economic Incorporation	Domestic Bargaining
Trajectory	Nation-State	Periphery	Indirect Rule

Figure 1 Three Waves of Late Ottoman Historiography

Modernization Approaches

Modernization approaches entered the Ottoman field after the institutionalization of area studies in post-war America. Cold war and decolonization played a critical role in this transformation. Both historic events confirmed the universal credentials of Western development and provided a favorable political environment to replicate that experience in the non-Western world. Around the same time, anthropologists and political scientists were documenting the momentous steps taken towards national integration, reaffirming the belief that the nation-state model was desirable and working for the rest of the world. Historians of the Middle East followed suit.[3]

The major impact of post-war world order on Ottoman historiography then was to put Western experience at the center of analysis. As Bernard Lewis aptly put it, the story of the Middle East and the Ottoman Empire should be told as the Western impact and the domestic response to it.[4] The historical dynamic that turned the Ottoman world upside down was the economically advanced, technologically superior, and culturally dominating Western world. Departing from the earlier conclusions of military historians though, modernizationists viewed the West as a civilizational asset with universal nature. In this view, the West was to be emulated and drawn upon to arrest imperial collapse.

With this perspective in mind, modernization authors put special emphasis on episodes of top-down imperial transformation. Accordingly, the proclamation of Tanzimat (1839) became the most credited event in late Ottoman historiography.[5] By creating a modern bureaucracy, building a new economic infrastructure, and strengthening cultural ties with the West, Tanzimat is seen as the landmark event that allowed the Ottomans to embrace Western modernity.[6] Earlier reform efforts of Selim III and Mahmut II are also noted as key moments of change and received justification for expanding the modernization ideal.[7]

The unveiling of a reformist thread produced a cyclical understanding of late Ottoman history. While the Ottoman state was moving towards progress and civilization, the undercurrent would be a reactionary backlash. Every major Westernizing reform was to be followed by a conservative reaction. The reformist Sultan Selim III was killed by a "mob" that opposed his new ways; the Tanzimat period was followed by the reign of the absolutist Abdulhamid II; and the Second Constitutional Period (1908–1918) was threatened by an Islamic upheaval in the capital city. Presenting late Ottoman history as a struggle between Westernizing reformers and conservative forces, first-wave authors endorsed the agenda of the former group.

That political agenda was modernization, which was believed to be the most critical process in late Ottoman history.[8] Synonymous with Westernization, it was top-down in format and bureaucratic in nature. Imperial reforms in the fields of higher education, administration and the military were highlighted to make the case that the Ottoman experience began to converge with the historical development of the West. Subsequently, the grand narrative of late Ottoman history turned into a list of achievements towards establishing state-led modernity, giving disproportionate attention to the secularization of education, modernization of bureaucracy, and Westernization of public life.[9]

Confusing legislation with implementation and state transformation with societal practice, the modernization school found a political agency to be named as vanguards of Westernization. This was the burgeoning bureaucratic class. Graduated from modern schools and blended with Western ideals, reformist intellectuals and army officers are thought to be a class in themselves. Belonging to the universe of 'middle class' revolutionaries at the turn of the century, they were better organized than their Iranian counterparts and had more access to state institutions than their Russian contemporaries. The Ottoman reformists were then assigned a historic mission: to save the Ottoman state from political collapse and transform Turkish society via a top-down Westernization project.[10]

With bureaucratic agency in charge, modernization historians were ready to announce the ultimate direction in

Military strengthening. The First Battalion of the First Infantry Regiment of the Imperial Guard.

Ottoman–Turkish history: to reach the level of (Western) civilized nations. This was the main historical outcome of interest. In fact, to the surprise of modernization historians, this is exactly why this type of history writing is not historical but rather theory-driven.[11] The idea is to explain the successful modernization of the Turkish nation–state by reconfiguring the Ottoman past. As such, late Ottoman history served an ideological purpose with no independent narrative of its own; that is, to provide a selective background to the emergence of modern Turkey.[12]

Nonetheless, first-wave scholarship was fully aware that the Westernization project of the bureaucratic class was not the only political option on the imperial agenda. There were ethno–religious and regional interests throughout the empire, and rival perspectives took hold in the palace and among the ranks of Ottoman bureaucracy. The modernization school viewed these multiple sites of opposition as a threat to imperial existence and named them a reactionary front. The opponents of bureaucratic transformation were blamed in particular for blocking the path to modernization and progress and keeping the empire backwards. At this point, political opposition and cultural dissent acquired a regime-threatening and trajectory-shifting meaning in the modernization discourse.

Political opposition operated at two levels in the analysis. First, top-down reforms create resentment and alienation with the 'ignorant' masses and the self-interested provincial elite. This type of social reaction was shown with reference to the Tulip Era, the Tanzimat period, and the Second Constitutional Revolution.[13] Second, as Niyazi Berkes formulated it very cogently, ideological rivalries divide the imperial elite into two camps, as reformists and traditionalists.[14] From a modernization standpoint, the worst-case scenario was the building of alliances between the two layers of opposition, which would destabilize the state and threaten the Western trajectory. The best-case scenario required the purging of conservatives from the upper echelons of the state and securing a trouble-free periphery with quiescent masses.

One of the innovative arguments of the (later) first-wave studies then was to introduce intra-elite tension and center-periphery conflict as the key elements of regime change in the Ottoman Empire. Both instances represented fundamental disagreements about the content of the state which were fought over (the scope of) Westernization. Hence, the more the Ottoman–Turkish state was Westernized, the weaker it became in the eyes of its subjects.[15] Consequently, the modernizing Ottoman–Turkish state lost its legitimacy in society, turned Islam into an ideological shield of the periphery, and created a major divide among the ranks of the political elite. Şerif Mardin thinks that this type of public alienation started in the final years of the late Ottoman Empire and accelerated with the founding of the Turkish Republic.[16]

Overall, modernization accounts provided us with a monocausal explanation about political change in Ottoman history. Late Ottoman history came into motion with Western impact and became a derivative story about the defensive modernization of the imperial state.[17] Periodization choices, state-centered analysis, and the evolutionary idea of becoming a modern society were based on a selective and ideologically-catered reading of Ottoman history. We are told over and over again that top-down modernization is the only successful project on political change and state formation in the Third World, reflecting the teleological vision and universal bias of the modernization school.[18]

Modernization approaches left a huge deal of late Ottoman history outside. Even the key story of imperial reforms which was at the heart of the modernization narrative was covered via legislation attempts in Istanbul, leaving the larger question of state-society relations missing in the analysis. Pre-occupied with high politics in the capital, there was no room for a spatial perspective in the modernization analysis.[19] As such, the major problem with this approach is that it ignored the diverse record of imperial subjects across the Ottoman territories and assumed its convergence along modernization lines towards the end of the century.

Two other points are worth mentioning that will open up the discussion to the macro models in late Ottoman historiography. The first point is about the content of modernization. By attaching modernization to Westernization and Ottoman state practices, first-wave authors presented a restricted version of Ottoman modernization. Not recognizing a public sphere outside the realm of the state, modernization views were silent about the ways in which social classes, families, religious communities, provincial elite, and the janissaries negotiated with modernity. Second, the impact of the West was primarily discussed as a set of values and novel state practices, leaving world economy at the sidelines of the modernization story. Macro models would address these challenges and explain the late Ottoman world with reference to global processes.

Macro Models

Macro models entered Ottoman Studies in a different political environment. The fracturing of the modernization project during the 1970s replaced the idea of progress with economic backwardness. Third World elites blamed global capitalism and its domestic allies for the failure and lost their political motivation to catch up with the West. Sharing this anti-capitalist and anti-imperialist rhetoric, popular mobilizations began to challenge domestic and international hierarchies. Masses demanded economic rights for peasants and workers, and asked for complete independence from imperialist domination. Yet, the globalization wave of the 1980s solved these conflicts in favor of global forces and powerful groups, terminating inward-looking, state-centered and populist regimes.[20]

Dependency school, social history research and world-systems perspective reflected on these developments and built a strong intellectual and theoretical base alternative to modernization approaches in Ottoman historiography. Macro models agreed on capitalism as the causal story, viewed introduction of foreign trade as the turning point, registered global economic incorporation as the main historical process, and presented political peripheralization as the final outcome in late Ottoman history. As such, this brand of Ottoman history-writing provided an economic analysis of the late Ottoman scene, attaching imperial processes to global structures of power and inequality.[21]

Capitalism was the causal dynamic that transformed the Ottoman Empire during the nineteenth century. The Ottoman state had seen its provisioning system fall apart and its fiscal options severely restricted by Great Power politics. Meanwhile, capitalist expansion transformed the Ottoman economy, creating richer hinterlands, bigger port-cities, and a strong merchant class organized around global commodity chains. The capitalist entry to the Ottoman soil also brought new conflicts-which were fought over economic resources, worker rights and trade networks. Linking capitalism to loss of political sovereignty, class formation, and social resistance, second-wave studies confirmed the constitutive role that world economy played in the late Ottoman Empire.[22]

Macro models view the Ottoman entry to the world economy as the turning point in late Ottoman history. According to the dependency school, the Anglo–Ottoman trade treaty (1838) set up an unfair trade regime and introduced concession politics to the Ottoman Empire.[23] Protecting the interests of foreign creditors against a bankrupt Ottoman state, the Public Debt Administration (1881) served a similar purpose. It consolidated the alliance between imperialism and finance capital, intensified the class conflict between the bourgeoisie and the bureaucracy, and siphoned off revenues from Ottoman territories.[24] Taken together, these turning points pushed late Ottoman history into a new historical path whose key variables would be world economy and imperialism.

Integration to world markets sealed the new direction in late Ottoman history. Foreign trade increased more than ten-fold throughout the century as the Ottomans sold a variety of cash crops to world markets and bought European manufactured products in return. Meanwhile, foreign direct investment upgraded the Ottoman infrastructure (such as railroads and harbors) and expanded the volume of foreign trade. Starting with the Crimean War (1854), loans from European money markets came with high interest and commission rates, leading to foreign control over Ottoman finances in the long run.[25] Notwithstanding the debates about economic growth and European imperialism, macro models share the conclusion that world markets put the Ottoman economy on a new footing during the nineteenth century.[26]

A major consequence of economic integration was modern class formation. As Reşat Kasaba demonstrated in the context of western Anatolia, the expansion of foreign trade created a new merchant class.[27] The domestic bourgeoisie had three main features: it was urban, non-Muslim, and connected to the world economy. Despite the disagreements between dependency and world-systems schools over its economic position and political significance, the non-Muslim bourgeoisie thesis shared the ethnic division of labor idea that assigned economic occupations to non-Muslim communities. It was from this intellectual base that Charles Issawi announced the economically predominant position of non-Muslims in the Middle East during the nineteenth century.[28]

Not fully satisfied with this approach and under the influence of peasant studies, Ottomanists began to explore agrarian patterns during the 1980s. Landholding became the complementary strategy to search for the class structure of late Ottoman society. Most of the intellectual energy was spent on tracing the regional applications of the Ottoman Land Code (1858) to assess the impact of agrarian relations on class inequalities and regional differences. Three conclusions stand out from this research: (1) the rise of large landholdings (*çiftlik*s) played a limited role in the Ottoman incorporation to the world economy; (2) landholding patterns shaped several hierarchies at the local level; and (3) agrarian structure is partly responsible for creating different political outcomes in the Middle East during the twentieth century.[29]

Second-wave studies also explored Ottoman responses to world economic integration. Disputing the economic-decline thesis of the dependency school, Şevket Pamuk documented dependent development in the Ottoman economy with foreign trade. He showed how integration to world markets took place via middle peasantry, departing from colonial and informal empire cases. Manufacturing also survived the European onslaught and became more competitive in certain sectors at the height of the European expansion. The labor composition, cheap import of raw materials, and local preferences in particular helped to secure a domestic manufacturing base.[30] This historical trend was especially strong in Ottoman Bulgaria, trading towns of eastern Anatolia, and the cities of northern Syria.[31]

Around the same time, social historians placed workers and peasants at the center stage of late Ottoman history. Donald Quataert documented the struggle of tobacco producers in eastern Black Sea region who resisted the Regie Company and its global economic allies. In a similar fashion, port workers blocked European economic interests in Salonica and Beirut for a considerable time. In the political sphere, the port-guild helped the Committee of Union and Progress to establish firm control in the cities by organizing collective protests against foreign products. In all the cases above, social historians portrayed workers and peasants as "agents of change," who directed their anger against Western imperialism and shaped domestic politics in the closing years of the empire.[32]

Economic incorporation soon created political consequences. This is what dependency and world-systems perspectives respectively called colonization or peripheralization of the empire.[33] Despite the differences in theoretical language, there was agreement over the historical outcome of interest. Out of global economic incorporation, a weak Ottoman state emerged. The Ottomans lost their sovereign status when dealing with the European states, gave in to the systemic logic of the global economy, and possessed limited power vis-à-vis their own subjects during the nineteenth century. This tripartite model stemmed from the structural position that the Ottoman Empire occupied within the world economy, which was better than a colonial spot but hardly a match for the "semi-peripheral" status of imperial Russia.

With waves of anti-imperialism growing stronger during the 1970s, the Turkish historiography was intellectually and politically ready to show the end of the drama; how European economic domination and peripheralization of the Ottoman state were dismantled at the closing years of the Ottoman Empire by the Turkish Revolution. Focusing on the war decade (1912–1922), dependency authors such as Feroz Ahmad and Zafer Toprak documented Turkish nationalist economic policies during World War I, which terminated the European privileges in the economy that had been secured through Ottoman capitulations.[34] Favoring a vanguard-agency explanation (that turned Westernizing elites into anti-imperialist revolutionaries), the idea was to put economic independence at the center of modern Turkish state formation.

Economic independence. Removing the French post box in Jerusalem with the abrogation of capitulations.

In sum, macro models worked through a conflict paradigm and viewed late Ottoman history as a site of double struggle waged between the Ottoman Empire and the West on one side, and the non-Muslim bourgeoisie and the Ottoman bureaucracy on the other. This reading was backed up by an economy-centered and class-based approach that put world economy at the center of analysis. Macro positions differ in interpretation. Dependency approaches argued for economic backwardness and loss of political sovereignty, while economic and social historians documented dependent development and searched for sites of local resistance to the global economy. Finally, it was the world-systems perspective that traced the rise of an autonomous bourgeoisie in conflict with European traders and the Ottoman bureaucracy.[35]

There were two major problems with macro models in late Ottoman historiography. First, they operated with a mono-causal account of history, and second, they failed to show how economic structures persist over time. The former meant entrusting the world economy with full authority to determine turning points, historical processes and long-term outcomes, while the latter missed the opportunity to view economic incorporation as a networked activity that needs to be reproduced in an ongoing fashion. Furthermore, by restricting the debate to economy and class and distrusting the state-centered agenda of the modernization school, macro models overlooked a major Ottoman development. This was the often slow, always uneven, and largely negotiated process of imperial consolidation.

By shifting the focus to state–society relations, it is the bargaining perspectives that would bring the experience of distant imperial lands to the center of late Ottoman historiography during the 1990s.

Bargaining Perspectives

The rise of bargaining perspectives in late Ottoman historiography is deeply influenced by global changes. The most important development in this regard is the decline of the nation-state framework. It shattered elitist regimes and made class politics less of an option. Global flows, identity politics, and the erosion of domestic sovereignty further revealed the limits of nation-state experience. Meanwhile, the relative decline of the Western world provided momentum for the emergence of regional patterns which have started to redefine hierarchies between the West and the rest in recent years.

The sea-change in Ottoman Studies took place with the demise of Eurocentric analysis. Under new scholarship, the historical experience of the West appeared less hegemonic than it was assumed in the past. Current research has demonstrated that Western dominance was limited in scope, and benefited from Eurocentric discourses to keep its hegemonic position.[36] In light of these findings, modernization approaches and macro models have lost their intellectual appeal in Ottoman historiography. They have been superseded by historical narratives that give agency to the Ottoman state and local actors in the making of the modern Middle East.[37] Subsequently, Ottoman modern state formation emerged as the new intellectual vista in the field.

Third-wave historiography began its (neo-) revisionist task by unpacking Ottoman state formation during the nineteenth century. The new scholarship has shown that state centralization destroyed the unchallenged position of local notables, political participation in imperial bureaucracy consolidated the power of provincial elite, and the late Ottoman state produced overarching imperial ideologies for legitimacy and survival. Taken together, these studies confirm the multi-layered character of the Ottoman state-building process. In doing so, they successfully explain the long-term stability of the Ottoman regime and unveil the brokered nature of Ottoman state formation.[38]

The brokered nature of Ottoman state formation was most evident in the realm of provincial bureaucracy. Micro studies went to great lengths to show how local interests occupied the new imperial posts and determined the degree of bureaucratic efficiency on the ground. In this respect, third-wave scholarship provided ample support to the idea that the more the late Ottoman state became bureaucratic, the more it was taken over by local interests at the provincial level. Not surprisingly, then, the number of politically influential families never exceeded a dozen in several Ottoman cities in the post-1860 period.[39]

Contemporary historiography has also documented severe competition over economic resources. This trend was especially visible in border provinces where there were strong local leaderships and weak central authority.[40] Elsewhere in Palestine, the Nablusi elite also kept a significant share of the agricultural surplus in the region.[41] Meanwhile, business partnerships materialized between provincial bureaucrats and the local elite, and tax-farming played an instrumental role in attaching provincial interests to the imperial center. Current research concurs that the central state left a considerable amount of the surplus in the provinces, which in turn allowed it to negotiate better with the locals.

The other area of state-society interaction in late Ottoman times was the ideological domain. The Ottomans invented new forms of political legitimacy and upgraded their institutions in order to consolidate imperial rule. The former were put into use by the pan-Islamic policy of Abdulhamid II. In an often-cited book, Selim Deringil discussed several 'imperial legitimation' mechanisms that garnered support from the Muslim public.[42] The latter became effective when imperial institutions accelerated the Ottomanization of the imperial elite.[43] With its Islamic content and prospects for social mobility, imperial schooling produced a generation of 'late Tanzimat men' who reconciled their local identity with an Ottoman public persona and gave their allegiance to the Ottoman state.[44]

Further support for the bargaining model came from the decentralized eighteenth century. Discussing tax-farming relations in Diyarbakır, Ariel Salzmann portrayed a city that was well-managed by the local elite. The local leadership supported regional interests, yet had strong fiscal ties to the center.[45] Karen Barkey took the same argument one step further and associated tax-farming interests with burgeoning provincial civil society in the Ottoman Empire. She showed how a major beneficiary of the tax-farming world, the Karaosmanoğulları family, established close ties with foreign merchants, provided protection to local groups, and became an influential community leader in western Anatolia.[46] More broadly put, institutional readings underline a

Bargaining with locals. Ali Ekrem Bey in Beersheba, 1905.

symbiotic relationship between the center and periphery, which in turn sponsored "federative structures" in the Ottoman Empire.[47]

Contemporary historiography is in agreement over the long-term trajectory of late Ottoman history: indirect rule that required the cooperation of local intermediaries. Fiscal and economic resources were shared between center and provinces, local politics was dominated by the provincial elite, justice and education were under the helm of communal forces, and even the Ottoman army recruited soldiers from irregular forces in the frontiers. By focusing on the question of domestic rule, this type of Ottoman history reading departed from modernization approaches and macro models that respectively discussed bureaucratic restoration and peripheralization of the empire under the decisive impact of the West or the world economy.

The turning points of late Ottoman history represent the collapse of the bargaining model. Third-wave authors suggest that top-down reforms of the Tanzimat reversed the path of negotiation and destroyed center–periphery alliances. Postcolonialists blame in particular the new civilizing imperial ideology, which fostered a socially elitist, politically centralist, and culturally modernist project. In line with this approach, Ussama Makdisi recently argued that the Ottoman reform movement not only produced primordial identities in Lebanon but also projected a backward east that coincided with distinct religious (heterodox Islam), ethnic (Arab), and spatial (Western Asia) identities.[48]

The other "suspect" in third-wave historiography is the Second Constitutional Period (1908–1918). Şükrü Hanioğlu sees the Young Turk Revolution as the outcome of a successful military insurrection that harbored a conservative political agenda.[49] More broadly put, postcolonial criticism raises two important points about the closing years of the Ottoman Empire. First, the late Ottoman state was more Turkish, elitist, and centralist than was previously assumed. Second, it was the social Darwinism of the Young Turks that initiated reactive Muslim nationalisms, a Christian exodus, and the collapse of the Ottoman Empire.[50] In this view, the final episode of late Ottoman history is associated with negative change, where the modernizing bureaucratic class destroyed imperial diversity in the name of modernity and the state.

In sum, the recent success of third-wave historiography has to do with shifting the intellectual focus to imperial state-building. These studies demonstrate with ample evidence that the key to understanding the late Ottoman world rests upon discovering the specific political bargains between the Ottoman state and social actors.[51] Accordingly, imperial mechanisms that sustained or terminated the material and ideological ties between the central state and its peripheries received special attention. By unpacking state–society relations, this research program also advanced a far-reaching conclusion: that it was primarily Ottoman decision-making and Ottoman institutional choices that shaped the Middle East during the eighteenth and nineteenth centuries.

Current accounts still differ from within. The major point of contention concerns the nature of the late Ottoman state. Microhistory studies portray a low-capacity Ottoman state and depict the centrifugal forces as agents of history. The institutional school gives more credit to Ottoman state power and underlines the alliances between local elites and the central state. The emphasis is put on mechanisms that secured the livelihoods of the center and the periphery. The postcolonial approach presents the late Ottoman state as a powerful actor, practicing exclusion towards frontiers and 'heterodox' social groups. The key here is the ideological transformation of the late Ottoman state.

By way of conclusion, I will identify three major weaknesses pertaining to third-wave research. First, there is the issue of scale. Local history studies concentrate most of their energy on the local unit, yet underestimate the constitutive impact of imperial and global factors. Second, current research from postcolonial positions confuses the sociological imagination of the bureaucratic class with the reality on the ground, assuming an Ottoman state with instrumental rationality and extensive capabilities. Third, the institutional analysis credited tax-farming with positive sociability and political outcomes, failing to report its spatial and temporal limitations and overlooking its negative impact on Ottoman modern state formation during the nineteenth century.

Conclusions

Late Ottoman historiography provided us with narratives of change. Modernization approaches highlighted state-led transformation; macro models traced burgeoning class antagonisms after capitalist penetration; and bargaining accounts demonstrated the tacit contract between Ottoman state and society. Accordingly, modernization research successfully documented the reformist-state tradition. With a different intellectual question, macro models turned the attention to the impact of the world economy, underlining its political costs and unintended positive consequences. More recently, bargaining perspectives emphasize the negotiated character of Ottoman state formation and hint at its demise with the rise of the modernist bureaucratic project during the second half of the nineteenth century.

The state of the late Ottoman field is promising. Old-fashioned political history is increasingly dominated by postcolonial and institutional questions; social history gave its bottom-up approach and agency perspectives to local history; economic history leaned towards global comparisons; and world-systems research became more process-oriented. As a result of these developments, the historical continuities between eighteenth and nineteenth centuries are brought to light;[52] the research on the Ottoman Empire extended to geographically "non-core" imperial territories; and the nation-state divides that compartmentalized the Ottoman field for so long have weakened recently.[53]

However, key issues remain unsolved in the Ottoman historiography. An important point that deserves mention is the lack of intra-Ottoman perspectives. By subscribing to what Charles Tilly called propensity explanations, Ottoman scholarship views history with reference to purposeful actions of social actors. Late Ottoman history is evaluated through the lens of bureaucratic elites or provincial leaderships. In this formulation, imperial history becomes a narrative of conflict or cooperation between the two units.[54] This account is problematic for two reasons: first, it reduces Ottoman history to a state-centered narrative expressed within a center–periphery framework, and second, it leaves no room for domestic comparisons to capture intra-Ottoman variation.

The other difficulty in the historiography is the overwhelming presence of mono-causal accounts that explain late Ottoman history with reference to a single dynamic. It was the West with the first wave, world economy with the second, and imperial consolidation with the third that provided the analytical framework for constructing late Ottoman narratives. By proposing a single direction for the whole empire, this view misses the interactive causal complexity that shaped the late Ottoman scene during the nineteenth century. Methodologically speaking, then, late Ottoman historiography cannot successfully explain the different constitutive roles played by the Ottoman state, global processes, and local actors at the same time.

As a remedy, I will suggest that we need historical accounts that address intra-Ottoman variation and operate with multi-causality. These accounts need to be spatial and comparative on one side, interactive and process-based on the other. They should historicize the contribution of the Ottoman state, qualify the European impact, and view local actors as powerful networks in the region. This kind of approach holds the potential to bypass binary accounts, avoids proposing a single path of imperial development, and de-emphasizes the centrality of political elites in the capital.

Following these guidelines, the rest of the book will show that imperial trajectories can offer a way out to go beyond dualistic narratives and state-based accounts in late Ottoman historiography. The next chapter turns to the eastern Mediterrean littoral first and presents the Ottoman coast as a distinct regional path during the nineteenth century.

CHAPTER 2

COAST

The coastal path was a social formation that came into being during the nineteenth century. It rose to prominence with expanding world trade and epitomized increasing specialization in the global economy. Yet the coast was more than a geographical niche that attached the Ottoman Empire to the core centers of the world economy. Port-cities served as social spaces that connected the Ottoman coast to global networks, fostered middle-class alliances, and initiated new forms of political conflict. Accordingly, reformist ideals, a broad public sphere, and modern class politics were integral components of the coastal experience during the nineteenth century.

This chapter discusses the coastal trajectory in the late Ottoman Empire. It starts off by emphasizing the role of the world economy in the making of the coast and shows how domestic actors were the major beneficiaries of economic integration. Later, I explore the rising hegemony of middle classes in the port-city that was shaped by global flows and manifested itself in municipal authority and the port-city press. The final section examines new forms of political conflict on the Ottoman coast that increasingly took a class-based character at the turn of the twentieth century. My overall argument is that the coastal model fostered a distinct historical experience in western Anatolia and the eastern Mediterranean littoral during the nineteenth century.

The Making of a Globally-Connected Economy

The historical origins of the coastal path go back to the second half of the eighteenth century when the Ottoman Empire became incorporated into the expanding European world economy. Benefiting from political decentralization and economic stability, governors of coastal cities and powerful notables responded to the rising demand from Europe. They channeled peasants' surplus to foreign markets and provided protection to long-distance trade.[1] The major port for Ottoman exports, Izmir, was selling mohair yarn, silk, cotton and wool to the industrial markets of Europe.[2]

Ottoman integration into the world economy, however, proved to be temporary. Ottoman political actors neither complied with the principle of predictability in economic exchange nor altered the production process towards further commercialization. Tax-farmer landlords and provincial governors instead squeezed the peasants as much as they could after paying the central state a fixed revenue. Furthermore, as the historical record of Acre confirms, political leaders always kept a distance between European merchants and local economic processes. As a result, no mono-crop hinterlands emerged in Ottoman territories.[3] This short-lived model ended with the Napoleonic Wars that disrupted trade links between the Ottoman Empire and Europe.

The trade framework was radically altered in the eastern Mediterranean after the 1820s. The major difference was the meteoric rise of local-capitalist agency. Occupying an intermediary position in Ottoman–European trade relations, non-Muslim merchants eliminated local Muslim groups from economic competition in long-distance trade and enjoyed organizational advantages over Europeans. Two-way connectedness was the key to non-Muslim commercial ascendancy on the Ottoman coast as it enabled urban interests to forge economic ties with global actors and the hinterland at the same time. It was against this background that the Greek merchants of western Anatolia sustained their monopoly over the import trade of the region throughout the century.[4]

Domestic commercial interests thrived on the coast because of their locally-embedded character.[5] Non-Muslim entrepreneurs relied on social ties to reorient economic life towards foreign markets, have easy access to credit, and share market information. As such, ethnicity, religion, common place of origin, and kinship provided reliable channels for economic exchange that required mutual trust and cultural compatibility in the region. When the Ottoman foreign trade increased more than ten-fold during the nineteenth century, not surprisingly, hometown connections were instrumental to the operation of silk-reeling factories in Mount Lebanon, and marriage alliances and ethnic money markets supported commercial activities in western Anatolia and Salonica.[6]

Well-functioning regional networks guaranteed the economic success of coastal merchants in the long-run. They sealed the alliance between urban interests and middle peasantry and preserved the competitive character of Ottoman markets. In doing so, they pushed aside other forms of economic integration. There were no European monopolies, white-settler colonies, or powerful rural interests on the Ottoman coast. Instead, non-Muslim entrepreneurs dominated silk exports in Lebanon and Bursa, controlled tobacco and manufacturing businesses in Salonica, and traded in a variety of cash crops in western Anatolia. As of 1913, there were more than two hundred locally-owned silk-reeling factories in Lebanon.[7]

The structuring of coastal markets around extensive trade networks tied economic performance to network control. The Greeks of western Anatolia proved to be the most capable agents in this regard, as they combined "the operations of a carrier, merchant and moneylender."[8] This was not an available option for others. Lebanese Christians depended on French capital for credit; Armenians invested much of their capital in land; and the Jews of Salonica had limited access to the Macedonian hinterland.

Seen in this light, the major obstacle that the Europeans faced on the coast was their inability to penetrate to local networks that controlled commodity movements on the ground. As late as 1889, Banque Imperiale Ottomane, the major institution that financed foreign trade operations in the empire, had only twelve branches established throughout the provinces, leaving the task of commercialization in the hands of domestic groups.[9]

If embeddedness kept European interests at bay, economic diversification allowed the local actors to stay competitive on the coastal economy. This was a wise strategy to distribute risk in a business environment that operated with limited capitalization, vertical communal networks, and no active state support. Historically speaking, the urban bourgeoisie of the Ottoman Empire functioned as a usurer group in the hinterland, traded in cash crops for the world economy, and invested in urban manufacturing and real estate. This experience set the Ottoman coastal firms apart from their counterparts in the West, where the economic rationale had been to dominate a global commodity market or an entire domestic economic sector with state support and/or capital accumulation.[10]

Coastal merchants began to diversify their economic portfolio with the end of the Great Depression in the 1890s. They found it profitable to invest in manufacturing as the major Ottoman port-cities experienced rapid demographic growth. The changing business strategies of Allatinis in Salonica reveal the new economic orientation of the port-city that was now driven by urban demand. The famous Jewish entrepreneurial family first shifted their economic operations from tobacco to a flour mill, then built a brick factory towards the end of the century. The Greek bourgeoisie of Izmir followed suit, investing in manufacturing, construction and food-processing. They opened breweries, steam-flour mills and soap factories, and specialized in producing durable goods such as bricks and roof tiles.[11]

The Ottoman coastal bourgeoisie also invested in real estate and were engaged in land speculation.[12] Izmir and Beiruti merchants transformed nearby commercial centers and invested money in booming towns. Subsequently, places like Jaffa, Haifa, Mersin and Samsun grew from isolated spots into regional port-towns.[13] They received immigrants from outside and posed a serious challenge to the larger port-cities in the eastern Mediterranean.[14] The latter development not only exposed the fragile nature of Beirut's commercial hegemony (because of its small size, late-comer status, over reliance on silk economy, and the presence of regional competitors) but also signaled a new wave of agricultural commercialization in the region.

Seen in this light, port-town development in the Ottoman Empire was a consequence of deepening integration with the world economy. Mono-crop hinterlands emerged on the Çukurova plain with cotton, in the eastern Black Sea region with tobacco, and on the Palestinian and Syrian coasts with orange and silk production.[15] Farmers in northern Palestine and southern Marmara planted olive trees more aggressively during this time. Meanwhile, bulk goods from inland regions began to reach coastal markets.[16] New forms of economic integration soon required coastal outlets closer to centers of production. Subsequently, Haifa was upgraded into an important port for grain exports, Hawrani wheat reached to the port of Acre, and Aleppo began selling wheat and barley through Iskenderun.

The Ottoman state and European merchants helped the coastal economy in different ways. By pursuing centralization policies, the Istanbul government undermined the "old elite" who had monopoly over the rural surplus and the urban economy. The Porte stopped cooperating with the powerful ayans, eliminated their fiscal base by discontinuing the *malikane* system, and crushed them militarily. The end of the "kapı dynasties" also meant that double taxation and internal duties that were associated with tax-farming interests received a severe blow by the 1840s.[17] As such, it was the earlier elimination of corporate actors by the central state that made free trade possible on the Ottoman coast.

Rise of regional port towns. The construction of Haifa Railroad.

Unable to penetrate the hinterland and having been forced to cooperate with the domestic non-Muslim bourgeoisie, the European merchants limited their operations into certain areas. They financed foreign trade through capital-intensive investments and provided physical amenities to the expanding Ottoman port-city. The extension of Beirut's harbor (1890–1895) and the construction of the 110 km Beirut–Damascus road (1863) with the French capital exemplified this trend.[18] Still, the major contribution of the Europeans to the coastal trajectory lay elsewhere. As was the case with Chinese treaty-ports, Europeans upheld a legal framework that kept the free movement of commodities intact in the eastern Mediterranean and guaranteed privileges of extraterritoriality to non-Muslim merchants in the Ottoman Empire.[19]

After a few decades, the coastal economy paved the way for middle-class hegemony in western Anatolia and the eastern Mediterranean littoral. The next section introduces the actors, mechanisms, and ideologies of cosmopolitan rule on the Ottoman coast towards the end of the century.

Middle Class Hegemony

The rising economic fortunes of domestic merchants coincided with the burgeoning ideological hegemony of a professional middle class in the port-city. Journalists, lawyers, pharmacists, doctors and the literary elite expanded the boundaries of the public sphere on the Ottoman coast and created middle-class networks in western Anatolia and the eastern Mediterranean. Mostly from non-Muslim origins, they became opinion leaders, cultural mediators and enthusiastic reformers in the Ottoman world. The professional careers of Butrus al-Bustani and Khalil al-Khuri in nineteenth-century Beirut nicely illustrate the historical evolution of Ottoman middle classes under the influence of global flows on one side and domestic realities on the other.[20]

The port-city intellectual possessed a distinct social habitus in late Ottoman society. He was cosmopolitan but local, and pro-reform but neither anti-state nor against community. Ottoman middle classes viewed modernization from a locally-embedded perspective and searched for the "right balance" between the local and the global. This position was crystal clear in the way western consumption patterns, communal identities, and gender relations were discussed in the Ottoman press.[21] Still, as "rooted cosmopolitans," they did represent a challenge to existing communal hierarchies, the increasing power of the Ottoman state, and the European imperialist project.

Middle classes were genuine reformists on the political front. Starting with the 1860s, they campaigned for representative political institutions and formulated the idea of an imperial fatherland. Both proposals were compatible with the ideals of the Tanzimat and did not promote political nationalism.[22] Instead, the reformist discourse was built on the notion of imperial solidarity and envisioned "concentric homelands (*vatans*)" within the Ottoman universe. While the former point shaped the Young Ottomans' thought, the latter provided the ideological arsenal for Lebanese Nahda Movement.[23] Accordingly, imperial reform remained the main reference point for middle class politics until the Great War.

The short-term impact of the middle classes was on the city. As Beirut, Salonica and Izmir became contentious with the weakening of communal ties and the birth of class politics, middle classes responded to social polarization of the urban space in two ways. First, they argued that social justice in the Ottoman city could be achieved by reconciling private interest with the public good. Promoting a solidarist view of society, they shied away from radical organizations despite their support to the workers' cause. Second, they were skeptical of the idea that religion could foster a harmonious society.[24] They saw public charity, donations and education as major ways of helping the poor, the unprivileged and the community in modern times.

The other troubling issue from a middle-class perspective was the urban question. Alarmed by the pace of demographic change, port-city intellectuals campaigned for increasing control over the city space. They called for a new social order that would not be disrupted by seasonal migrants and vagabonds on one side, and disease, crime and prostitution on the other. Towards the end of the century, modernist and moralizing discourse turned migrant bachelors into "usual suspects" in Istanbul whereas the socially-delinquent became an easy social target in Salonica.[25] As of 1900, expert rule was in the making in the port-cities of the Ottoman Empire.[26]

The middle classes operated in modern institutional settings to make their case for political reform, social peace and urban renewal. As the political career of Hamdi Bey in Salonica (1893–1902) nicely illustrates, with a distance from the central state the municipality was a perfect environment for showcasing middle-class proposals. The municipal councils would allow professional groups to experiment with reformist projects and test the practical limits of their social ideals. Local politics was also about power. Professional groups registered their rising social status in their own community, challenging the traditional hegemony of religious leaderships.[27] For instance, the city municipality of Beirut was controlled by merchants and reformist intellectuals who closed the doors of city governance to rural notables and religious dignitaries from 1868 to 1908.[28]

Professional groups also used ideological instruments to win the public over to its modernization agenda. The flourishing port-city press was very influential in this regard, as it introduced middle-class ideas to Ottoman society. Keen interest in science and technology, the idea of an Ottoman public, and catching up with the civilized world were the major aspects of middle-class thought. The civilizing/modernizing perspective was also evident in literary works such as short-stories and novels that imagined a new type of Ottoman citizen. For instance, as Ilham Khuri-Makdisi recently showed, theater was tied to middle-class radicalism in several Ottoman port-cities at the turn of the century.[29]

Symbol of modernity. Clock Tower of Izmir.

Middle-class rule was built on cosmopolitan space. The cosmopolitan setting was the result of pull migration, and came into being with demographic change in the eastern Mediterranean. With their dynamism and diversity, port-cities attracted Europeans with an opportunistic agenda and appealed to immigrants with social ties in the city.[30] Merchants from Europe, missionaries from the West, social relatives from hinterlands, and seasonal laborers from less prosperous regions consolidated the multi-ethnic and multi-religious character of the Ottoman coast.[31] As such, the Armenians of eastern Anatolia not only made a fresh start in Istanbul around the 1890s, but also contributed to the cosmopolitan ideal.

Cosmopolitanism. Galata Bridge connecting the old and the new in Istanbul.

Port-city cosmopolitanism was crucial for middle-class rule on the coast. The coastal classes did not have to compete against an entrenched urban-Muslim bloc or face a challenge from predatory rural leaderships. Moreover, the modern setting gave the professional groups a historic opportunity to build their ideological hegemony in the port-city. It was only then that the educated groups formulated a reformist agenda and spread it through powerful media such as the press. Taken as a whole, the cosmopolitan terrain provided the necessary social space, the right set of institutions, and the free flow of ideas that elevated the middle classes into the leadership position on the Ottoman coast.

Middle-class attempts to create a peaceful port-city under the helm of merchants and professionals did not go unchallenged, however. The next section turns to coastal contention and shows how communal conflicts in the hinterland, tensions of hegemony in regional port-towns, and worker protests in major port-cities were part and parcel of the Ottoman integration into the world economy.

Economic Contention

Spoils of world trade set a new basis for distributional conflicts in the eastern Mediterranean world. The initial stage of conflict was the hinterland, where economic actors and the politically-connected elite clashed over land and commercial agriculture during the first half of the nineteenth century.[32] The disagreement pitted the independent-commercial peasantry against tax-farming notables, each side promoting an alternative economic model for the hinterland. Druze landlords and Maronite peasants fought for two decades in Lebanon, leaving behind eleven thousand dead in 1860. In Macedonia, non-Muslim merchants pressured Muslim landlords to put more land into commercial use.[33] In both situations, economic struggle was framed along communal lines and perceived as such.[34]

The Ottoman coast achieved political stability after the 1860s when the land question was resolved in favor of economic actors. The setting up of a Maronite-dominated autonomous entity pacified Mount Lebanon and strengthened the market-oriented agricultural units. In western Anatolia, the earlier centralization efforts of the Ottoman state consolidated the middle peasantry and contained the conflict between weakened Muslim landlords and non-Muslim city merchants. The main outcome of "agrarian peace" was the transformation of the hinterland into a cash-crop producing region for the world markets, which brought economic prosperity to the Ottoman coast.[35]

The boom cycle of the world economy unleashed new forms of conflict on the Ottoman coast towards the end of the century.[36] The first signs of communal tension appeared in the hinterland when Muslim interests began to rival non-Muslim cash-crop producers in western Anatolia and Mount Lebanon. This came after the demographic expansion of port-cities and increasing worldwide demand for grain, as both developments turned trade in bulk goods into a profitable business. Subsequently, grain merchants in Mount Lebanon and Muslim economic interests from the outskirts of western Anatolia began to thrive in the

Trade in a multi-cultural setting. A Christian merchant from Aydın, a rabbi from Izmir, and a Muslim merchant from Manisa, 1873.

hinterland. Merchants of Afyon, who were selling livestock products to Izmir, were members of an upcoming Muslim bourgeoisie around 1900.[37]

Nonetheless, the uprooting of economic hierarchies in the hinterland did not translate into political action with the exception of Macedonia.[38] The real challenge came from the cities, where urban conflict took the form of ethno–religious rivalry in regional port-towns and class competition in major port-cities. The former trend was visible in Haifa, where rapid demographic expansion following the economic boom made the power struggle between Christians and Muslims contentious. Still, the political outcome was more of convergence along status lines. While upstart merchant families with non-Muslim backgrounds were able to intrude upon the ranks of municipal and administrative councils, Muslim households were involved more with trade and land speculation.[39]

It proved more difficult, however, to contain communal confrontations in other Ottoman port-towns. This was especially the case when outside migration threatened local interests and the new commodity chain favored one local group over the other. Accordingly, Jewish immigrants clashed with Arab residents in Jaffa, the Greeks of Ayvalık got into conflict with recently settled Muslim population, and the mono-crop economy of tobacco separated the interests of Greek middle classes from their Turkish counterparts in Samsun.[40] In this vein, regional port-towns increasingly looked like microcosms of cosmopolitan port-cities, yet hosted competing communal coalitions with no clear pattern of leadership and vision.[41]

Class conflict defined political contention in major Ottoman port-cities at the turn of the twentieth century. Worker activism developed in two ways. First, small-numbered modern workers clustered around transportation, food-processing, and tobacco industries engaged in collective action. Mostly from non-Muslim backgrounds, they formed unions, made strikes, and benefited from the socialist politics of the day. For instance, the Tobacco Workers Union of Salonica had more than three thousand members at the time. The new worker vision asked for better economic prospects and implanted a radical political culture in the eastern Mediterranean.[42]

The other contentious group in the port-city was the predominantly Muslim workers with guild backgrounds. Historically speaking, guild members enjoyed monopolistic control over their trade and received political support from the central state. This was especially important for port-workers who had leverage over the city economy and now played a crucial role in foreign trade operations. Faced with the gradual decline of the guild organization, workers were mobilized into action. Supported by the local authorities and public at large, they were able to protect their traditional workplace autonomy and occupational rights against European capitalists. This was especially the case in Salonica, Beirut and Istanbul, where foreign investors tried to eliminate them in the name of economic profitability.

Workers in the two camps had different agendas and organizational capabilities. The main goal for modern workers was to expand economic rights. They used a new type of organization (union) to make a claim, and gradually incorporated a progressive discourse to build a more egalitarian future. Meanwhile, the guildworkers' class action sought to protect privileges and routines in the occupation. Collective mobilization aimed at protecting a weakening organization (guild) from ultimate collapse and utilized the vocabulary of a just social order. The resistance of Jewish porters to the rebuilding of Salonica's seaport clearly demonstrated that the latter group was primarily interested in preserving the status quo rather than initiating progressive social change.[43]

Despite internal divisions, there was still a common ground that defined worker activism across the port-cities of the eastern Mediterranean. First, operating in multi-ethnic and multi-religious settings, worker mobilizations were mostly cosmopolitan in nature. Second, class identity was strongest in places where workers experienced class in non-workplace environments.[44] This was especially the case in Salonica and Alexandria where neighborhoods were segregated along class lines. Third, workers received support from the radical wing of the middle classes. Acting as brokers and certifiers, the vision of the middle class was solidarist in nature and demanded state intervention in the name of the public good. The perspective of Gabriel, the activist physician of Anatolian Railway Company, reflected this approach.[45] Finally, there was the world of small trades.[46]

The class struggles of workers belonged to a larger set of conflicts that were waged for getting a larger share from the global economy. Having forced out the Ottoman state from the winners' table through capitulations (which could possibly take its share by taxing economic transactions), the influential parties left in the game were European capitalists and non-Muslim merchants. They benefited the most from Ottoman integration into the European world-economy by selling foreign products to Ottoman customers and controlling access to domestic markets. While local actors had the upper hand in the age of free trade (1820–1870), the age of imperialism put European firms into an influential position for the next fifty years of the Ottoman coastal economy.

At the turn of the twentieth century, the Ottoman bourgeoisie and European merchants confronted a political problem bigger than workers' resistance. This was the reform agenda of the Ottoman bureaucracy.[47] The Ottoman state wanted to tax the port-city more effectively and deal with its legitimacy deficit on the coast.[48] The latter was especially urgent for two reasons: first, European consuls exerted a considerable pressure in city affairs, and second, economic hierarchies worked against Muslims especially in Izmir and Istanbul.[49] After a brief moment of joy, the leaders of the Second Constitutional Revolution had to invent new ways for changing internal hierarchies in the port-city.

Conclusions

The world economy transformed the Ottoman coastal space in substantial ways. It upgraded coastal enclaves into major

Connected to global flows. Pera neighboorhood in Istanbul.

port-cities and connected them with commercial hinterlands directed towards global markets. Nonetheless, Ottoman port-cities did not emerge on a purely accidental basis. With no major imperial roles prior to global incorporation, places such as Beirut and Izmir proved to be perfect fits for market transformation. At this point, political intervention from outside was also crucial. The Ottoman state cleared the way for global capitalist integration by eliminating political brokers, and Europeans secured the free trade regime by protecting extra-territoriality and commodity movements on the Ottoman coastal space.

Three historical developments in particular gave a unique character to the coastal experience in the Ottoman Empire. First, the coast slipped away from effective imperial control. Shaped by free-trade, the coastal path was controlled by non-Muslim merchants whose economic fortunes depended more on the global economy than the Ottoman state. Port-cities amassed enormous economic wealth, which elevated the cosmopolitan bourgeoisie to a leadership position, gave birth to a nascent civil society, and sponsored a discourse of urban autonomy.[50] Accordingly, Ottoman port-cities became multi-ethnic and multi-religious environments characterized by an expanded public sphere and a variety of global connections.

Second, a strong domestic middle class consolidated the distinct character of the Ottoman coast. Despite the resillience of communal boundaries, merchants and professionals created a novel setting in the eastern Mediterranean which was shaped by the priorities of a modernizing urban group. Middle class rule was locally-embedded, materially strong, and ideologically hegemonic. From the port-city press to merchant houses, from municipal councils to social clubs, it was their perspective that counted the most on the Ottoman coast. As such, coastal middle classes were not simply trade diasporas of an economic sort but rather influential domestic actors who successfully transformed a region in their own vision.

Third, the Ottoman coast experienced new forms of collective action. There were acts of communal violence in the hinterland, tensions of hegemony in port-towns, and class struggles in the port-city. At the turn of the twentieth century, political contention was primarily a consequence of world market integration and social struggles were fought for getting a bigger share from the spoils of global economy. It is also worth mentioning that collective claim-making installed a novel democratic tradition in the port-cities of the eastern Mediterranean. The key was the expansion of the public space, that became increasingly accessible to the less privileged, economically powerful, and the socially aspiring.

Moving from littoral zones to inland regions, the next chapter discusses the evolution of the interior trajectory in the late Ottoman Empire.

CHAPTER 3

INTERIOR

Inland regions experienced a different kind of imperial reality during the second half of the nineteenth century. With no foreign intervention threat and limited presence of global markets, the Ottoman Empire was able to shape the interior around its own priorities and transform the state into a hegemonic force in the region. State transformation also confirmed the privileged status of urban intermediaries who participated in the modernizing Ottoman state, and secured Muslim domination in regional economy and local politics. Over time, inland regions became firmly attached to the imperial universe.

This chapter discusses the making of consensual rule in central Anatolia, Syria and Palestine. The first section examines the social composition of the local elite who governed inland regions through expanding bureaucratic structures. In the second section, I show how market opportunities were tied to the state, and consolidated the power of an urban Muslim bloc. The third section explores political contention at the elite and mass levels, and concludes that the provincial Ottoman state became the epicenter of patrimonial conflicts for competing households in the post-1860 period.

An Urban Muslim Bloc

The making of an urban Muslim bloc was the result of Ottoman state expansion in the second half of the nineteenth century.[1]

State centralization changed the social composition of the local elite, redefined the bargaining terms between locals and the central state, and provided powerful groups with a new institutional setting to coordinate their interests. The key instrument that the Ottoman state used for this purpose was provincial bureaucracy. By holding access to power, imperial bureaucracy served as the premium site for gaining (or losing) elite status in inland regions. Subsequently, a new ruling bloc emerged whose priorities, values and interests developed in relation to the Ottoman state.

Ottoman centralization made a qualitative difference in the interior. It crushed powerful locals on an individual basis, yet reintegrated them into the imperial framework as part of an influential bloc. Post-centralization Syria illustrates well the new political environment through which the central state interacted with locals. The Ottomans eliminated powerful rural interests in the north, settled nomads and heterodox religious groups in central areas, and reorganized the whole region by creating the province of Syria in 1865.[2] The imperial state also overcame popular resistance to taxation and began to protect cities and long-distance trade better.

If centralization policies regrouped the local elite, state expansion diversified it in the long run. By extending the bureaucratic arm of the state and continuing the Egyptian practice of provincial councils, the Ottomans broadened the universe of political brokers in major towns and cities. They elevated merchants and *ulema* into the ranks of the Muslim bloc. Accordingly, seven of the twelve families that governed Damascus at the second half of the nineteenth century had neither privileged background nor public visibility prior to 1860. On a similar ground, twenty-five *ulema* families that controlled religious institutions (*ilmiye*) in Nablus began to penetrate the Ottoman civil bureaucracy around the same period.[3]

The urban political order took hold in the interior with the elimination of powerful rural interests. The political fall of the bedouin leader Aqil Agha in Galilee and the destruction of the toll-collecting Abu Gosh family in the Jerusalem Mountains completed the pacification of Palestine.[4] Centralization in central Anatolia and the sedentarization of tribes in Syria were already accomplished before 1860. The relocation of Kozanoğulları family from Taurus and Amanos Mountains by the imperial state not only secured safe passage from Anatolia to Syria but also showed Ottoman determination to increase public security and terminate rackeeters in inland regions.[5]

Merchants, tax-farmers, absentee landlords and local bureaucrats soon merged into a common economic front. Their main goal was to impose an urban order in the countryside. They tried to take the surplus from the peasantry, buy large tracts of land in the countryside, and use frontier populations as cheap labor. The commercial interests of Damascus in Hawran and the employment of Alawites in Hama estates clearly demonstrates that interior economic organization favored urban-Sunni groups over rural and heterodox others.[6] For this purpose, urban interests also built alliances with the middle peasantry and village entrepreneurs (*shaddads*) in order to eliminate district *şeyhs*, clan leaders, and bedouins from economic competition.[7]

The other challenge to urban Muslim rule came from non-Muslim groups in the cities who prospered from long-distance trade. One setting for such conflict was Aleppo where East-West trade created severe economic competition between foreign-protected non-Muslim merchants and domestic entrepreneurs during the eighteenth century.[8] Muslim interests rose to the challenge by fighting non-Muslim commercial groups, the equality discourse of the Tanzimat, and the penetration by the Europeans into inland regions. The failed conversion agenda of missionaries, limited landholdings of Europeans, and the relative absence of non-Muslims in the public sphere all testify to the political success of the Muslim bloc in the long run.[9]

The Muslim bloc was firmly attached to the late Ottoman state. Office-holding was the main mechanism through which

Eliminating the rural hero. Bedouin.

the provincial elite accumulated economic wealth, boosted political power, and reproduced community leadership positions. On the economic front, a bureaucratic post was the key to securing tax-farms or buying large tracts of land in the interior. In political life, administrative councils, with their control over conscription and tax collection, served as sites of elite coordination and built social reputation for the influential households. In religious matters, Sunni dominance was guaranteed by the Ottoman state, and the *ulema* needed the Ottoman provincial bureaucracy for politically-empowering judicial posts and revenue-generating pious foundations (*vakıf*).

The political durability of interior regimes can be further shown by examining the case of Damascus more closely. Philip Khoury found that there were only 12 families who controlled the higher echelons of politics in the city after 1860.[10] Tracing the economic power of the same social group from sharia court registers, James Reilly concluded that they paid more money and made larger sales than the rest of the society in irrigated agricultural regions.[11] Elizabeth Thompson underlined the bargaining power of the Muslim bloc. Representing the prestigious families, the High Advisory Council of Damascus was able to represent the common interests of the local elite against the central state during the early years of Ottoman centralization.[12]

Assisting the group interests of the ruling bloc as a whole, Ottoman provincial bureaucracy was critical for a member of the local elite to serve his household. This was especially true when top bureaucratic jobs came with a variety of positions. These posts typically went to the members of the extended family, and created a network of political clients ranging from religious orders to neighborhood constituencies. For instance, an influential political figure in the Abdulhamidian era, Ahmad Izzat Paşa, placed his son Muhammad Ali Bey to serve as the only Arab Ottoman ambassador abroad and secured bureaucratic posts for his brother, brother-in-law and nephew. Historically speaking, the Paşa's behavior was no exception.[13]

With the implementation of the Ottoman Land Code, land ownership became an important instrument for consolidating local leadership in the interior. Accordingly, political brokers such as Jabirizade and Mudarriszade of Aleppo and Husaynis of Jerusalem turned into absentee landlords in major cities.[14] A similar trend was visible in low-profile towns with less economic potential. Landed interests dominated Safad after Ottoman centralization, absentee landlordism was fundamental to the social formation of Hama, and Cabbarzades emerged as the strongest family in Ankara who controlled politics, tax-collection, and several administrative positions in the province.[15]

The interior order had local origins as well. More than anything else, this was about the family. The family operated as an economic unit and as a social-hierarchy setter in the region. Beshara Doumani has shown that even before Ottoman centralization, male lineage in *vakıf* property was jealously guarded to protect the economic survival of the family.[16] During the late Ottoman period, elite families pooled resources through marriage. This development strengthened economic and social ties between secular and religious members of the local elite and confirmed the political oligopoly of a few select households. Moreover, by concentrating power in the hands of a small group, the family contributed to the hegemonic character of interior order.[17]

Ottoman power reached its climax in the interior at the turn of the twentieth century. With modern education expanding during the 1890s, the imperial state promoted an inclusive Ottoman identity and provided career opportunities to a large group of people.[18] Ruth Roded suggests that 83 percent of graduates from state schools in Syria joined the Ottoman bureaucracy.[19] Subsequently, imperial institutions became the primary means through which a younger generation of local elite kept its privileged position and talented Muslim men from modest backgrounds had quick access to social mobility. While the former group preferred to go to law school and imperial school for civil service to take up positions in the civil bureaucracy, the latter typically chose military careers and joined the Ottoman army as officers.

In sum, the making of consensual rule in the interior was the historical outcome of two related processes. First, Ottoman institutions transformed the status groups of the eighteenth century into an urban Muslim bloc with common interests. The new intermediaries began to control political positions, economic

Training the imperial bureaucrat. Imperial School of Civil Service students (Mekteb-i Mülkiye-i Şahane).

Training the imperial bureaucrat. Law School Building.

Istanbul style. An upscale Damascus home at the turn of the century.

resources and religious authority. Second, institutional innovation deepened the partnership between locals and the state. As of 1900, late Ottoman rule was firmly embedded in cultural repertoires and imperial routines that revolved around modern schools, "state Islam", the Ottoman army and the provincial state. The rising cultural influence of Istanbul on Damascus is a powerful reminder of the kind of hegemony that the Ottomans were building in the last decades of imperial rule.[20]

Turning from politics to the economy, the next section shows how the Muslim bloc was the major beneficiary of regional economic integration in inland regions.

Creating Regional Markets

Interior economic life was resilient to global influences. The world economy and its agents were rather inconsequential actors in the interior, playing only a marginal role in these regions. This was historically the case for two reasons: first, the political intervention of the late Ottoman state shaped economic processes, and second, a strong Muslim bloc dominated regional markets. As such, political rents and domestic markets determined the evolution of inland economies in the second half of the nineteenth century. In this section, I first examine the impact of the Ottoman state on the economy, and then discuss regional market integration with reference to bulk goods and local manufacturing.

The closest link between interior economy and imperial politics was tax-farming.[21] Tax-farming was a fiscal policy where the ruler delegated state functions to social interests because of revenue crunch or limited bureaucratic capacity. Starting with the seventeenth century, domestic reform and costly wars forced the Ottoman state to farm out tax-collection rights and rely on tax-farming as an internal borrowing strategy. From the perspective of lender groups, though, tax-farming offered a unique opportunity to accumulate wealth in the Ottoman world. It was a legitimate form of business that did not necessarily challenge the (short-term) objectives of the central state.

Tax-farming practice operated in three stages in the Ottoman Empire. Moneyed interests funded the enterprise in the capital; high-ranked bureaucrats sealed the deal with the central state; and politically-connected local interests collected the revenues from the tax source in the provinces. In this respect, investors were organized as an economic network and brought in economic capital, political muscle, and effective oversight to "lease and run" the fiscal unit.[22] The Muslim bloc dominated the last spot in the operation and emerged as a powerful subcontractor class in the interior. Unlike coastal merchants and autonomy-seeking frontier leaders, they had monopoly over local processes and proved to be trustworthy partners of the central state.

Landholding was the other economic area where state resources in private hands made a difference in the interior. When the Ottomans decided to liberalize the predominantly state-owned property regime after 1858, the application of the Land Code gave those with imperial authority a historic opportunity.[23] The Muslim bloc had easy access to information, resolved land disputes in their favor, and bought, sold and registered property with ease. Broadly speaking, land accumulation occurred at the expense of tribal groups in the countryside and the poor in the cities who resisted the idea of private ownership and lacked financial resources respectively. As a result, large landownership consolidated especially in Syria.

The Ottoman state intervened in the economy in more direct ways as well. The provincial bureaucracy tried to level the playing field in favor of local merchants by obstructing the free-trade regime of 1838. This economic strategy, which relied on states of emergency, internal tolls and domestic monopolies was successfully put to use in northern Iraq and Baghdad.[24] The Ottomans also provided inland regions with a new infrastructure when they had enough state capacity. In the provincial capital of Syria, this meant a modern transport network, a redesigned downtown area, and new bazaars to boost economic activity.[25] More generally, though, increased public security was the main Ottoman contribution to regional trade and commercial agriculture in inland regions.

Interior economic life was resistant to foreign penetration. This partly had to do with the Muslim merchants' ability to transform the countryside.[26] They lent money to peasants with interest (*salam contracts*), made speculative purchases in advance (*daman*), established control over cultivation rights, and commodified uncultivated (*mahlul*) and unoccupied (*mawat*) lands through sharecropping arrangements. Local merchants utilized social relations to accumulate economic power. Kinship, social ties and marriage alliances were crucial to exchange information, establish business partnerships and extend credit. It is no wonder then that the entire soap production of Nablus was in the hands of ten local families by 1900.[27]

Interior economies took important steps towards regional integration at the end of the nineteenth century. The Muslim bloc was at the center of this transformation. Interior merchants forged urban–rural links, controlled overland trade, and built dense trade networks. Historically, they were able to connect large cities such as Aleppo, Baghdad and Damascus, dominate the vibrant trade networks of the Fertile Crescent, and direct Damascene trade towards Ottoman and Egyptian markets.[28] Around 1900, Palestinian merchants were expanding towards southern Syria, connecting the region to the Palestinian economy. As Suraiya Faroqhi rightly pointed out, Muslim merchants focused on regional trade rather than building an international orientation.[29]

Inland economies were based on bulk agricultural goods, the two main categories being cereals and livestock. Growing markets for bulk goods and faster modes of transportation facilitated the emergence of a grain belt during the 1890s. 75 percent of cultivated land was allotted to grain in Palestine, 90 percent of agricultural taxes came from wheat and barley in Mosul, grain surpluses of Hawran found their way to the cities of Syria, and grain shipments from central Anatolia reached a record level in 1902. Subsequently, a larger portion of bulk goods from inland regions began to arrive in regional markets at the turn of the twentieth century.[30]

Economic transformation strengthened mid-size market towns. The latter emerged as regional textile centers, sold manufactured products to the hinterland, traded with large "caravan" cities, and established strong connections with burgeoning port-towns of the coast. Konya merchants used Mersin as an outlet for grain exports, Homs relied on Tripoli to connect to foreign markets, Hama turned into a regional textile center that produced cheap cotton fabrics, Nablus rose in the interior hierarchy as a soap manufacturing center, and Mosul became the "breadbasket" for northern Iraq and southeastern Anatolia. Meanwhile, Aleppo, Damascus, and Baghdad stayed at the top of the economic hierarchy as they forged economic networks among themselves and functioned as regional distribution centers.[31]

With increasing commercialization of bulk goods, grain merchants emerged as influential figures in the interior. They were especially strong in central Anatolia, Syria and Baghdad. The key to their success was urban markets. Merchants of central Anatolia reached the two largest markets in the Ottoman Empire after the construction of Anatolian Railway, selling wheat, barley and cattle to Izmir and Istanbul. With no competitors around, regional merchants also monopolized urban markets in inland cities. On the political front, grain merchants became important allies of anti-colonial, anti-cosmopolitan and nationalist projects and later joined resistance movements in Turkey and Syria.[32]

Manufacturing revived in inland regions during the last quarter of the nineteenth century. Despite pressures coming from the world economy and coastal regions, rising demand provided the incentive for local industries.[33] Domestic manufacturers were strong in east-central Anatolia and the urban centers of Syria. Accordingly, Tokat, Antep and Diyarbakır flourished as important textile towns in Anatolia. The weaving industry also boosted its production levels in Yozgat and Arapkir with British yarn. In Syria, the textile industry of Aleppo alone employed more than 200 merchants in 1908, and no less than half of northern Syria's textile output was consumed by Ottoman markets.[34]

Domestic manufacturers survived in regional markets. They operated on a low-cost basis, benefited from customer tastes, and targeted the lower end of the market. Textile merchants should be singled out in this regard. They used extensive chains of subcontracting, fragmented the production process, and benefited from low-wage labor. For instance, Kayseri merchants relied on the putting-out system, home loooms were extremely popular in Mardin, and declining piece rates sustained the economic viability of Diyarbakır merchants. As Donald Quataert points out, the major advantage that interior manufacturers enjoyed was the way they organized the production process.[35]

The other key to merchant efficiency was the use of a non-guild and unorganized workforce. Ottoman entrepreneurs targeted young, unmarried and rural women in particular.[36] According to one estimate, two-thirds of the workforce in the east-Anatolian textile industry belonged to this category. Non-guild and women's labor helped the manufacturers to lower production costs, enjoy a less-contentious laborforce, and sustain production levels in the long run. Subsequently, the Ottoman weaving industry captured a significant share of regional markets and flourished in inland regions at the height of European economic expansion.[37]

In sum, there was market integration in the Ottoman interior by 1900. Several trends characterized this process. First, market integration took place at the regional level, where the impact of the world economy was limited. Second, flexible manufacturing and commercialization of bulk goods were the economic forces that secured market integration in Anatolia, Syria and Palestine. Third, the Muslim bloc was the major beneficiary of economic transformation as the imperial state distributed assets (i.e. land) in a political fashion and provided a favorable environment to local interests.[38] The latter was achieved by preventing global actors and their allies from penetrating the interior scene.

Economic transformation soon created its own discontents. The next section turns to collective claims and examines the nature of political conflict in inland regions.

Patrimonial Tensions

With market integration, the Muslim bloc was challenged from outside. This was especially true for upcoming members of the elite group who rose in the interior hierarchy with economic transformation. Textile manufacturers and grain merchants had to deal with artisanal discontent and bread riots in the cities, both of which were directed against the winners in a new economic order. Still, the most important form of conflict was about elite rule in these regions. Members of the Muslim bloc competed among themselves to accumulate power, resources and prestige in interior society. This section first traces patrimonial tensions around the Ottoman provincial state, then examines the social consequences of market integration.

Factional politics defined social conflict in inland regions during the eighteenth century.[39] Janissaries and guilds fought religious groups and local notables on several occasions and turned Ottoman cities into political battlegrounds between rival social coalitions.[40] Around the same time, powerful governors campaigned for political autonomy from the imperial capital, keeping center–periphery tensions at the center-stage of local politics. After the 1830s, social conflict acquired a new element in the interior. Muslim interests opposed the intrusion of European capital and the rise of non-Muslim classes, and were mobilized in important inland cities such as Aleppo, Mosul, Nablus, Damascus and Maraş.

Communal mobilizations were products of rapid social change in interior society. Non-Muslim elites increasingly mounted an economic challenge to Muslim interests, the social safety net that protected guilds and the urban poor ceased to exist with the destruction of janissaries, and the Ottoman state started a policy of centralization after the withdrawal of Egyptian forces.[41] Soon after, the masses directed their anger against wealthy Christian quarters such as Judayda in Aleppo and Bab Tuma in Damascus.[42] They held the local allies of European interests accountable for the collapse of the old order, and blamed the Christian protégés for undoing Muslim privileges.[43]

Collective violence of the 1850s was the turning point for inland regions. It secured the long-term victory of the Muslim bloc at a time when non-Muslim merchants, rural racketeers, the Ottoman central state, and European economic interests were vying for power in Syria and Palestine. Muslim rule was consolidated in two related ways. First, local notables monopolized bureaucratic posts despite the egalitarian and centralist discourse of the Tanzimat, and second, they enjoyed the spoils of economic transformation. Both processes accelerated with the expansion of the Ottoman provincial state and the rise of regional markets, and subsequently sealed Muslim rule in the interior.

Having pacified their political rivals, members of the Muslim bloc competed among themselves to accumulate power. Urban politics then took the form of alliances and rivalries among different sections of the Muslim bloc. First, political and religious interests merged during the 1870s. They began to control key spots in the bureaucracy and evolved into a landed class, especially in Syria and Palestine. After the 1890s, an Arab-imperial class and manufacturer–merchants challenged the narrow boundaries of the ruling bloc. While the former group included the graduates of imperial schools, the latter consisted of merchant (*tujjar*) families whose power rested on regional markets.[44] Around 1900, the Ottoman bureaucracy was at the center of competition among three groups who subscribed to the Ottoman world but disagreed on the pace of social change and state penetration to the local.[45]

Viewed from a long-term perspective, political contention followed a certain pattern in inland regions from the eighteenth to early twentieth centuries. It first shifted from sectional conflicts to a communal platform during the 1850s, and later took the form of patrimonial tensions around the provincial state. Accordingly, the late Ottoman state increasingly provided the necessary political setting for competing elite actors to solve their collective-action problems regarding material resources and cultural schemas. The other interesting observation about interior contention is that the Muslim bloc was the main party in every social conflict in these regions. While elite contention was fought within the Muslim bloc, popular contention was directed against it.

The new Arab-Imperial elite. Maktab Anbar in Damascus after renovation.

The new Arab-Imperial elite. Students from imperial middle school in Aleppo.

Popular contention came to life with market integration. Unlike the political character of elite rivalries, it was primarily economic in nature. The revival of manufacturing initiated a fierce struggle between a resistant labor and an ascendant economic class. Eager to join the Muslim bloc, merchants and manufacturers welcomed the birth of new markets and viewed this development as an opportunity to rise up in the interior hierarchy. Yet there was an important obstacle to this political strategy. Ottoman labor resisted flexible production methods that distributed economic benefits in an uneven fashion. As the interests of artisans and masters became seperated and guilds began to crumble, artisans took action to protect their own interests.[46]

A wave of mass protests soon ensued in inland cities. Silk-loom weavers held a huge rally in Damascus in order to block the further reduction of piece-rates. The provincial capital city also experienced a wave of strikes by 4–5,000 journeymen weavers.[47] Collective protests were organized by semi-skilled artisans who worked in small workshops. They targeted master-turned merchants in particular, and confrontations did not necessarily involve other social groups on both sides. Guild background, spatial proximity, occupational solidarity, and informal social ties explain the highly disciplined character and the specific social agency of the protest movements.[48]

The economic dispute also revealed several points about the changing status of artisans in interior society. First, artisans could not benefit from the land-market boom in the countryside that characterized inland regions in the last decades of the nineteenth century. Second, as an urban group, rising agricultural rents that made life more expensive in the cities did not serve them well.[49] Third, artisans interpreted the new economic realities through what Ron Aminzade and Doug McAdam call injustice frames.[50] They felt betrayed since the old consensus between masters and the journeymen and its oversight by the state was terminated without their consent. Street demonstrations and marches reflected this state of mind and aimed at protecting shop-floor power in an age of labor market uncertainty.

Interior manufacturers prevailed over artisans in the long run. Contentious politics of the artisans was short-lived, stayed within the boundaries of a moral economy framework, and failed to create a class identity. There were several reasons for this. As

R. Bin Wong found out in the late Qing context, weavers' protests could easily convince merchants to take their business elsewhere.[51] The Ottoman artisan movement was also not certified by external actors. Artisans lost the historical protection of the state, and there was no middle class hegemony – as there was on the coast – to campaign for their cause. Finally, strict trade boundaries and the absence of a formal organization prevented them from establishing a durable labor movement with a broad social base.

The other contentious item that characterized inland regions was bread riots. James Grehan examined changing forms of protest in Damascus from the sixteenth to the nineteenth centuries and concluded that there was a decisive shift from the mosque to the court as the venue of contention.[52] Bread rioters blamed the local officials for economic injustices and asked the Ottoman state to protect public interest, regulate the market and penalize profiteers. During the second half of the nineteenth century, bread riots became a function of merchant speculation that created "artificial hunger" in the cities. Merchants allied themselves with the local authorities to control the wheat market.[53] The masses responded to "merchant greed" in several ways. Most notably, they staged violent protests in several Anatolian cities such as Kayseri, Sivas and Erzurum.[54]

In sum, interior contention was shaped by long-term processes of market integration and imperial centralization during the nineteenth century. Economic contention found its perfect expression in artisan protests and bread riots, which took a new turn with the revival of manufacturing and growing demand for bulk goods. Meanwhile, political contention turned the Ottoman provincial bureaucracy into the primary site for elite competition in Syria, Palestine and Anatolia after the 1860s. The Ottoman state defined the terms of elite conflict and provided the venues for its resolution. It is also worth noting that both types of interior contention were urban in character.

Conclusions

The interior trajectory came into being with imperial centralization, and reflected the priorities of the Ottoman state and the urban Muslim bloc. The Ottoman state held the key to political power, economic resources and religious authority in these regions. In turn, the Muslim bloc enjoyed an almost complete monopoly over these domains. Crystallized around insider–outsider politics, the Muslim bloc competed for power, resources and legitimacy. Towards the end of the century, the late Ottoman state penetrated further into the interior society. Imperial schooling, the Ottoman army and provincial bureaucracy served as powerful institutional tools that diffused an imperial identity. As Molly Greene rightly puts it, "the Arab elites were never more Ottoman than at the moment of the empire's dissolution."[55]

Still, it is worth mentioning that the interior path had its own internal differences. This was primarily a function of imperial integration. While the central state had the most say in Anatolia, local forces were strongest in Palestine. Syria fell somewhere in between. Not surprisingly, imperial education and mass conscription made the biggest impact in Anatolia whereas the Ottomans were content with the idea of circulating influential households in Palestine.[56] In Syria, the imperial state was able to diversify the local elite and gave them some kind of imperial mobility.

In sum, if the coast represented the globally-connected regions in the Middle East, the interior belonged politically, socially and materially to the Ottoman world. The next chapter discusses the imperial experience in the frontiers where late Ottoman rule was weakest.

CHAPTER 4

FRONTIER

The Ottoman frontiers shared a common historical experience during the nineteenth century. Unlike the coast and interior, they were politically volatile, economically undeveloped, and demographically sparse regions. With limited state presence, the Ottoman frontiers were ruled by culturally distinct and politically autonomous leaderships that represented heterodox religious communities from non-Sunni faith.[1] In the age of imperialism, rising geopolitical rivalries also influenced political outcomes in Ottoman borderlands. This chapter surveys state formation patterns in eastern Anatolia, Iraq and the Arabian Peninsula, and suggests that it was the distinct nature of politics, markets and collective claims that consolidated thin rule in the Ottoman frontier.

The chapter is organized accordingly. The first section discusses the terms of bargaining between the central state and local groups, and reveals actual limits to Ottoman sovereignty. In the second section, my argument highlights protection rents in the economic sphere, that served the well-being of frontier leaders yet constrained Ottoman state-building efforts. Focusing on collective claims, the final section traces rebellious repertoires in the frontiers. I show how mass mobilizations aimed at protecting local autonomy against a centralizing Ottoman state.

Politics of Emergency

As the nineteenth century progressed, the Ottoman state faced a major dilemma regarding its policy towards the frontiers. While the centralization policies of the Tanzimat promised to extend citizenship rights, promote Muslim–Christian equality, and eliminate provincial powerholders from the scene, local resistance and the limited resources of the central state set practical limits to top-down imperial transformation. The growing ideological influence of Iran in lower Iraq, the Russian presence in the Caucasus, and the British diplomatic intervention in the Middle East further reminded the Ottomans of the delicate nature of state consolidation in the frontiers.[2]

As a result, Ottoman state formation took a different character in the frontiers. Combining direct-rule efforts with negotiation strategies on the ground, Ottoman governance rested on two contradictory principles: to penetrate directly into trust networks by accelerating the pace of Ottoman modernization, and to strike bargains with local leaderships for securing imperial survival. While the former agenda was formulated to initiate radical change in borderland societies, the latter tried to keep the status quo in place for Ottoman territorial integrity. As Maurus Reinkowski rightly pointed out, the late Ottoman frontier vision clearly reflected the "dilemma between the exigency of *realpolitik* and the ambitious Tanzimat reform policy."[3]

In line with the direct-rule principle, the Ottoman frontier policy acquired a new ideological element. This was the great transformation of the "periphery" by the Ottoman state. The "uncivilized" and the "backward" would be brought into the fold of civilization by freeing the East from the shackles of tradition, superstition and communal identities.[4] The civilizing mission found strong resonance among the educated members of the bureaucratic class who envisioned a modernist project to transform the frontiers. A former governor of Trabzon province and a high-ranked bureaucrat in the Public Debt Administration, Ali

Bey gave us an account of this sort for Ottoman Iraq towards the end of the century.[5]

The first step in the modernization agenda was to create a new security framework. As sea lanes and communication lines moved to the center of interstate competition, the Ottoman state tried to extend pacification, subdue local leaderships, and eliminate foreign intervention in the frontier regions. The forward move in eastern Arabia, armed clashes in Iraq, military operations in Yemen, and the construction of the 1900 km long Hijaz Railway along the Arabian Peninsula reflected this vision.[6] The Ottoman geopolitical mind was also evident in the bureaucratic correspondence between the frontiers and the imperial capital. Without a logistics revolution in place, the Ottoman officials asked for increased troop levels, faster means of communication, better technology, and more military supplies to improve the situation in Iraq and the Arabian Peninsula.[7]

When public security became less of an issue, the Ottoman state extended its operations into the bureaucratic front. Administrative centralization deepened imperial integration

Extending the imperial reach. Opening of Hijaz Railway.

and confirmed the rising authority of Istanbul over the provinces. Utilizing the Provincial Administration Law of 1864, the Ottomans incorporated the previously ungoverned regions into its political orbit, reduced the size of administrative units (Yemen, Iraq, Asir), and founded autonomous *sancaks* (Binghazi, Medina, Zor) directly attached to the center. The creation of Jabal Druze directorate in 1868, its division into three in 1900, and the assignment of non-locals to eastern Anatolia reflected the increasing attempts of the central state to monitor the frontiers and sensitive districts more closely.[8]

The reform package shifted to the economic front when measures of centralization were in place. The Ottomans promoted agricultural production, enforced the Land Code of 1858, and made several institutional changes for the sedentarization of tribes in Iraq.[9] The Ottoman idea was to create an infrastructure for material progress by clearing obstacles on public security and market economy.[10] Economic incentives would not only support commercial activity but also transform the social structures of the frontier in line with the interior model. In turn, the Ottoman state would benefit from increased tax receipts and political stability, both of which would contribute immensely to imperial strength.

The last item on the modernization agenda was to introduce state education to the frontiers. With a massive drive to open schools at the turn of the twentieth century, even in the distant province of Yemen, the Ottomans were educating 1600 students in 1901 most of whom were enrolled in one of the nine primary schools.[11] On Druze Mountain, the Ottoman state forced local leaders to close all foreign schools in 1889 in order to replace them with their state-run equivalents. On similar ground, the Ottoman Sultan came up with a tribal school initiative to buy loyalty from the upcoming generation of frontier elites by turning them into middle-ranking bureaucrats. Ömer Mansur from Ottoman Libya demonstrated how far a tribal school graduate could go in the state hierarchy by becoming a member of the Ottoman parliament during the Second Constitutional period.[12]

'Taming' the Ottoman frontiers. Tribal School (Aşiret Mektebi) students in Istanbul.

Despite its progressive rhetoric and short-term accomplishments, the modernizing reform package did not transform the frontiers. Ottoman performance was less than satisfactory when it came to installing a bureaucratic machinery that could monopolize violence, revolutionize economic life, and contribute to the ideological hegemony of the state. As Aziz Bey found out in Hudayda, the reformist bureaucrat had limited technologies

'Taming' the Ottoman frontiers. Tribal School (Aşiret Mektebi) students in Istanbul.

of control to govern Arabia, and there were domestic challenges coming from Yemen, Asir and Hawran. Military mutinies in Hijaz, economic discontent in eastern Arabia, revolts of tribes in Yemen, and the fiscal difficulties of implementing domestic reform in eastern Anatolia and Iraq further reminded the Ottomans of the significant gap between their resource base and state-building discourse.

There was also the issue of monitoring, which led to a typical principal-agent problem in the frontier.[13] Despite high rotation rates, overlapping jurisdictions and rival networks within the provincial bureaucracy, the Ottoman bureaucrat abused his power. He was unaccountable to the center, poorly paid, and faced insecure career paths. According to Christoph Herzog, 5 out of 11 governors who ruled Iraq (1831–1872) were deeply corrupt officials.[14] The opportunity window led to corruption and various injustices in eastern Anatolia, Iraq and Arabia, the central issue being the tax-collection process. In the meantime, the Sharif of Mecca and the ruling şeyh of Kuwait exploited the gap between local and central bureaucracies by buying off the local governors or forcing them to leave.

When the modernizing Tanzimat package failed, negotiation schemes gained ascendancy in the frontier. This was done through the pan-Islamic framework of Sultan Abdulhamid II during the last quarter of the nineteenth century. Like his Russian and Japanese contemporaries, the Sultan viewed the cultural identity of empire as an important ideological instrument to seal off the Western threat.[15] This is partly why his pan-Islamist project was supranational but statist, and deeply religious but confessional. Using Sunni Islam as a political medium, the Sultan's intention was to buy trust from the frontier where power and information asymmetries haunted the Ottomans for a long time.[16]

Formulated in broader terms, the negotiation model rested on the idea of piecemeal change rather than radical transformation, and aimed at keeping local leaderships intact rather than destabilizing them. In this respect, the inclusivist framework represented an alternative route to secure the political survival of the late Ottoman state. Divide and rule, hostage politics, political exile and imperial stipends were traditional policy tools that served this grand strategy. Abdulhamid's imperial agenda was also assisted by newly invented traditions. The Sultan bestowed imperial medals and sent robes of honor to frontier leaderships to secure elite loyalty to the Ottoman Empire.

Inventing traditions. Ali Ekrem Bey presenting robes of honor in Beersheba.

If the negotiation model laid out the basic principles for Istanbul-frontier interaction, the actual bargains between the two depended upon the relative strength of both parties on the ground, the immediacy of foreign threat, and the confessional composition of the region. Three regional patterns emerged. In the near frontier, the Ottoman state was able to mold political hierarchies in eastern Anatolia and northern Iraq via centralization. In the intermediate zone of lower Iraq and southern Syria, the central government penetrated local communities, yet could not transform them in its own image. In the far frontier, imperialist competition and a weak state presence allowed the local leaders of Arabia to bargain with the central state from a high ground.

In eastern Anatolia and northern Iraq, local rule shifted from a tribal leadership to a rural-religious class.[17] Mir Muhammed of Soran from Revanduz, Bedirhan Bey of Botan from Cizre and Mir Han Mahmud of Van from Müküs were the three leaders who resisted the most to Ottoman authorities. Nonetheless, as of 1847, all the autonomous Kurdish emirates were politically destroyed by the central state. *Şeyh* and *seyid* families benefited from the collapse and carved out an autonomous space as social brokers. Exemplified by the Nehri *şeyhs* of Şemdinli, the Sufi saints displayed common features: they came from outside, had prophetic genealogies, and functioned as community healers. Additionally, they excelled in arbitration of pasture disputes and blood feuds, and used marriage alliances, material gifts and *vakıf* property to consolidate power.[18]

Lower Iraq and southern Syria represented the intermediate zone in the frontier trajectory. The Ottoman state and weakened local leaderships clashed over the extent of centralization. There were two historical reasons for this: first, the Druze religious network in Hawran and the Shiite tribes in lower Iraq made it difficult for the Ottoman state to penetrate the region, and second, the local leaderships such as the al-Atrash clan in Druze Mountain and the Sadun family in Basra faced internal resistance during the 1890s. Combining coercion and negotiation, military campaigns and divide and rule strategies, the Ottomans responded to two-way resistance by making temporary pacts with the local elite and capitalizing on internal divides to extend gradual Ottomanization.[19] In Transjordan, the Ottomans displaced tribal leadership in the Ajlun and Balqa districts, yet could not repeat the same success in Karak and Ma'an further to the south.[20]

The relative power of the local elite was stronger in the rest of the frontier. Controlling Hijaz province, Asir and Yemen on the west coast, and the Gulf region on the east coast of the Arabian Peninsula, the local leaderships of the far frontier represented regionally-based, rival, and personalist household regimes. They possessed religious charisma, community-leadership roles, and tribal means of violence. Furthermore, using Great Power threat as leverage, the Sharif of Mecca, Saud of Najd, Idrisi of Asir, Zaydi imams of Yemen, and *şeyhs* of the Gulf coast were able to protect their autonomy.[21] With limited options available, the Ottomans tried to manipulate intra-household competition and rival claims to regional leadership in order to hold on to their thin rule in the Peninsula.

The Ottoman presence in the frontier was based on thin rule because of the limited institutionalization of the state. The central government worked hard to lure influential local actors into the Ottoman realm, albeit with limited success. The Ottoman state made a difference in the frontiers only when it implemented centralization and served ascendant local interests. This was especially the case in Transjordan, which was an extension of southern Syria. Meanwhile, the Ottomans had to deal with intact leaderships in the far frontier. As Yemen's political experience confirms, the central state had limited financial, human and coercive capabilities in these regions and faced strong local resistance.[22]

Imperial failure at the frontiers was also a product of short-sighted policy. The Ottoman state missed a golden opportunity to transform its frontiers when peasant uprisings shook Sason, Druze Mountain and lower Iraq. As a firm believer in the negotiation model, the Ottoman Sultan strengthened local leaders in northern Iraq, kept them in power in Druze Mountain, or ignored their de facto fragmentation in lower Iraq. Only in the face of international crisis, he considered changing the status quo and sent his confidants as "supergovernor inspectors" to eastern Anatolia and Iraq.[23] His main concern then was geopolitical. In contrast to the earlier reformist tradition laid out by Midhat Paşa, this vision neither tolerated provincial social change nor gave real responsibility to local administrations.[24]

Viewed from a long perspective, Ottoman state-building efforts failed in the frontiers during the nineteenth century. The next section turns to the economy, and shows how local leaderships were the major beneficiaries of a non-commercialized economic structure.

Collecting Protection Money

The economic forms in the frontier were in close affinity with thin-rule tradition in politics. The fiscal base of the region was limited, tax collection was costly, and military expenditures because of unabated insurgency caused major drains in the treasury. For instance, two-thirds of Iraq's expenditures were spent on security measures.[25] In the absence of a "Hobbesian state," markets also remained undeveloped and quality of life changed little compared to the rest of the empire.[26] Finally, the organization of frontier societies as distinct trust groups with easy access to means of violence allowed local leaderships to operate as competing predatory networks. They forced outsiders to pay as part of a customary rights framework, and demanded a community fee for their brokerage services.[27]

Violent entrepreneurs concentrated their activities on trade routes, communication lines and agriculture. Accordingly, the fate of long-distance trade and hajj caravans depended upon the transit dues extracted by the bedouin for safe passage in the desert. Tribes obstructed river transport between Baghdad and Basra, collecting fees from merchandise and human traffic. Stealing livestock occupied the number one spot on the racketeers' agenda in eastern Anatolia. The Wahhabi clans of Najd expected protection money from commercial centers and small peasantry. Even the Ottoman authorities were paying the tribes of lower Iraq and western Arabia for the upkeep of telegraph lines and railroad tracks respectively.

When protection rackets did not get their share, they stopped merchandise and human traffic all together. Despite the existence of a railroad connection to Medina, the number of pilgrims visiting the Holy Sites correlated positively with the safety of the pilgrimage route. The tribes were so powerful between Ma'an and Hijaz that passengers taking the train had to pay an extra fee for security reasons. At other times, tribes pillaged caravans, destroyed railroad tracks, and cut off telegraph lines in lower Iraq, Yemen and Hijaz province.[28] The next phase in the protest cycle would be to stage small-scale revolts in order to force the Ottoman government to meet local demands.

Looting was another resource-generating mechanism in the frontier. Targets were primarily chosen for their inability to protect themselves against outsiders. It is no wonder that the spoils of plunder mobilized the Anaza bedouins on the Damascus–Baghdad route, the Shammar in northern Iraq, the Druze in the Hawran plain, and the tribes of Najd in eastern Arabia. In a similar fashion, while the chances of booty sent 16,000 tribesmen from the Milli tribe to the gates of Diyarbakır, no less than 70,000 tribesmen joined Imam Yahya to take Sana'a. Serving as auxiliary Hamidiye forces, Miran, Milli, and Hayderan all utilized their de facto legal immunity to raid eastern Anatolia.

Urban interests, sedentarized populations, and social groups with limited access to protection adopted several strategies to block protection rents, especially in the near frontier. The urban notables of Diyarbakır informed the Sultan about a possible invasion threat by tribal forces. Armenian delegates from 24 towns met with state officials in the capital to stop raids and plunders.[29] In Süleymaniye, northern Iraq, peasants fled their villages to avoid plunder.[30] Framed as the "Kurdish question" in European circles, the Armenian peasants of eastern Anatolia complained bitterly about the Kurdish tribal chiefs who took their lands through semi-legal means and also demanded unpaid labor and arbitrary taxes.[31]

If protection rents were collected from outsiders, it was the community of believers who had to pay the membership dues. Located in the far frontier and operated as heterodox religious groups, the Zaydi Imams of Yemen and the Idrisi network of Asir expected a considerable sum from their own religious community. In alliance with tribes, the Sharif of Mecca also charged a religious fee. He took his share from the pilgrimage economy by controlling access to Holy Sites. Membership dues became a source of resentment in the long run and caused social upheavals in closely-knit heterodox religious communities by the last decade of the nineteenth century.[32]

Another major economic activity was smuggling. The practice was widespread throughout the Ottoman frontiers where seashore, impenetrable mountains, and long stretches of borderlands allowed entrepreneurs to evade customs and other forms of restrictions. Incompetent officials in border crossings, and local groups with social ties beyond the border, also contributed to undocumented economic activity. Smuggling created two important consequences for the Ottoman state: loss of revenue and militarization of the frontiers. While the former led to a smaller fiscal base, the latter prompted a more competent insurgency, both generating a larger drain from the central treasury.

Numerous observations confirm this historical pattern. North Albanian merchants traded in salt, guns and tobacco via Montenegro.[33] In eastern Anatolia, unregulated tobacco and salt trade with Iran continued unabated. In Yemen, export products such as coffee were channeled to British-controlled Aden to evade taxes. The seashores of Basra and Kuwait became hot spots for exporting horses and smuggling in guns. Iranian border regions around the Van province provided the necessary resources for Armenian nationalists to organize pockets of resistance against Ottoman rule.[34] On the shores of the Red Sea, the Hijaz Bedouins had no difficulty accessing thousands of smuggled handguns and rifles. Finally, the Saud of Najd and the Idrisi of Asir benefited from the courtesy of the Kuwaiti *şeyh* and the Italian state respectively to flex their muscle against Ottoman authority.[35]

There was regional variation in the frontier economy. The collapse of tribal confederations and the haphazard application of the Land Code created a new economic reality in the intermediate zone. Accordingly, lower Iraq was characterized by the forced departure of the absentee landlord Sadun family whose annual share from the peasants was now collected by the *sarkals*. This was a new social position that was tied to tax collection.[36] In central Iraq where the Ottoman Sultan owned much of the land,

Protection sellers. A member of Harb tribe (of Medina) with a rifle.

short-term tax-farming continued to be the norm and depended on the loyalty coefficient to the Ottoman state.[37] Tribal leaderships capitalized on the Ottoman Land Code in south-eastern Anatolia and registered vast lands under their names.

In all the cases above, the economic livelihood of tribe members was disrupted, yet not replaced, by market forces. The Land Code of 1858 did this by destroying existing land arrangements that were guaranteed under customary rights framework. Subsequently, short-term exploitation of the peasantry, introduction of new intermediaries, and seasonal labor migration became popular trends and created long-term outcomes. The rurally-dispossessed would be forced to go to big cities, supplying cheap labor in Turkey and providing political support to the revolutionary movements in Iraq.[38] In this respect, the migration of landless peasants (*fellahin*) into cities in Iraq, the employment of

Kurdish laborers on the Çukurova plain, and the transformation of Druze and Alawite communities into seasonal workers in Syria were part and parcel of the same historical transformation.

Economic forms began to shift towards the market in the near frontier. More than anything else, this had to do with the centralization efforts of the Ottoman state and the relative strength of urban interests on the ground. Sedentarization of tribes in southern Syria and the presence of small peasantry in northern Iraq also provided a favorable environment for market expansion. Accordingly, Mosuli, Damascene and Nablusi merchants penetrated to northern Iraq, Hawran and Transjordan via sharecropping arrangements and trade partnerships, intensifying conflicts over peasants' surplus in Jabal Druze, Jabal Sinjar, and Ajlun district.[39]

The other impetus came from growing demand for cereal, livestock and textile products during the 1890s. While northern Iraq was increasingly tied to production of livestock and wheat for Baghdad, Aleppo and Kerkuk,[40] Hawran became the grain silo for Damascus. Nablusi merchants came onto the scene in Transjordan with Ottoman centralization and seized the opportunity to connect Salt and other towns to the Palestinian regional economy.[41] Around the same time, eastern Anatolia turned into an important manufacturing site for regional markets as *seyids* and *şeyhs* replaced tribal leaders, and Armenian merchants made a powerful presence in the region.

There were two broad trends in the frontier economy in the long run. First, protection-money collection was most common in the far frontier where state power was weakest. The Arabian Peninsula represented the ideal type of frontier economy in which peasant customary rights and public security remained strikingly limited. Second, market integration spearheaded in the frontier when local demand was increasingly met from regional markets, urban interests were connected to the countryside, and the state had some capacity to provide security to the region. This was especially the case in northern Iraq and eastern Anatolia, followed by Transjordan and Hawran in southern Syria.

Another interesting observation about frontier economic forms is that they did not necessarily evolve around domestic markets or foreign trade. The decisive factors for frontier economies were limited state presence and the durability of closed trust networks. Both processes separately and in combined ways increased the transaction costs of economic exchange. As a result, while market integration and its urban economic actors made relatively little impact in the frontier, protection money collection and the subsistence economy remained as the major sources of income for pastoral federations.[42]

The next section turns to collective claims from the central state and explains how political contention was a constitutive force in the frontiers.

Rebellious Repertoires

The other causal mechanism in the making of the frontier path was contentious collective action. Fitting nicely with thin rule tradition in these regions, the frontiers produced the largest collective-action effort in the Middle East during the late Ottoman period. Driven by demands for local autonomy, frontier insurgencies had common features. They took advantage of low state consolidation, relied on patron-client ties, and turned into a mass movement via religious brokerage. This section discusses frontier resistance movements in detail and examines the unique advantages, specific motivations, and structural limits of insurgency in the region.

Frontier mobilizations followed a traceable pattern. They benefited from inaccessible terrain, utilized the superior information skills of the insurgents, and combined these advantages with third-party support and powerful movement brokers on the ground. Located on a rough terrain, frontier leaderships remained detached from the imperial capital for centuries. Mountains, highlands, deserts, strategic passes and narrow tracks were such topographical features that made Arabia, Yemen, Jabal Druze, and eastern Anatolia nearly impenetrable.[43] Even at the turn of the twentieth century, geographical constraint made military campaigns in the frontiers extremely costly with no apparent political gains.

Historically speaking, the Saud of Najd was so inaccessible in the heartland of Arabia that the Ottoman state had to contend with his expanding political leadership. In Yemen, where 12,000 feet mountain ranges with narrow passes connected the major cities, the Ottomans lost no less than 30,000 troops to take back Sana'a from the insurgents in 1905. Yet they still could not get the rebel leader Imam Yahya for logistical reasons. Tribes were skillful fighters in the desert whereas the Ottoman army was not a good fit for the task.[44] Strategic passes helped the Nestorians to survive in eastern Anatolia despite state pressure and attacks from powerful Kurdish tribal alliances that resulted in mass killings between 1843 and 1846.[45]

Frontier mobilizations relied on communal units to organize resistance movements. Operating as trust groups, frontier societies shared fictive-kinship bonds, a cultural–linguistic world, economic ties, and a common historical memory.[46] Yet, what turned "imagined" communal units into a unified opposition force was the duty of religious entrepreneurs. Religious leadership was able to transform symbolic groups into interactive networks for two specific reasons. First, they helped to create a distinct protest identity, and second, they brokered alliances beyond the core group by channeling information and providing legitimacy across tribal and clan-based boundaries.[47]

Brokerage was instrumental in creating an oppositional front, something that Ernest Gellner incisively called the tribal-Fronde alliance.[48] The religious entrepreneurs succeeded in this momentous task by promoting a discourse of resistance. For this purpose, they relied on the esoteric interpretations of Islam in Druze Mountain and promoted sufi-mystic approaches in eastern Anatolia. In Asir, central Arabia, and Yemen, their puritan message promised a return to the "Golden Age." In all of these situations, religious entrepreneurs successfully mobilized communities against Ottoman order by forging alliances across tribal lines and transcending local divisions in the name of religious ideals.

Religion was used as an ideological frame for mobilization in the frontier.[49] One important reason was confessional. Saud of Najd, Druze of Hawran, and Imams of Yemen represented heterodox brands of Islam which historically favored a mobilization approach. Despite its Sunni credentials, it was no coincidence that the Ottomans favored the widespread *Nakşibendi* network in eastern Anatolia to counter missionary influence. The other reason is clearly spatial. The call for pure Islam has been a trademark of frontier, rural and tribal Islam for centuries.[50] Inspired by North African Sufi traditions, the Idrisi movement in Asir was a perfect illustration of this trend.[51]

Frontier mobilizations benefited from third-party support. The neighboring state and imperial adversaries provided logistical support, military equipment and financial means to deepen hostilities in fluid border areas. During the late nineteenth century, Kurdish tribes of eastern Anatolia, the Shiite groups in the south of Baghdad, the Yemeni leadership, the patron of Kuwait, the Saud family, and the Armenian nationalist platform relied on resources provided by other states. Italian support to the Idrisi of Asir included the bombarding of the Ottoman coast (1911–1912).[52] In addition to foreign intervention, local governors also had a stake in influencing border politics.

Collective action in the far frontier was motivated by local autonomy perspectives. Hereditary leaderships expected to lose their customary rights if they did not act. They had no long-term institutional ties to imperial patronage and managed a clientele that could easily come under the control of the Ottoman state.⁵³ While Imam Yahya of Yemen insisted on dispensing tribal-sharia justice and collecting taxes to protect local autonomy, for the very same reasons, Wahhabi *ulema* and Zaydi jurists were at the forefront of opposition to an urban, Sunni and centralized Ottoman rule. At this point, arbitrary tax collection, fear of conscription, and the threat of an imposed Ottoman confessional identity united the populace with local leaders, turning contentious collective action in the far frontiers into an effective strategy for political bargaining.⁵⁴

The autonomy agenda was compounded by resistance to elite rule in the intermediate frontier zone. Tribal confederations and the religious elite faced internal opposition in lower Iraq and Jabal Druze by the 1890s. The key issue at stake was the erosion of customary economic rights after the implementation of the Ottoman Land Code. Facing problems of settlement/relocation, land use and water, peasants resisted the demands of "over-extraction" and organized small-scale revolts.⁵⁵ As a result, while the authority of the Sadun family over the Muntafiq tribes in Basra was terminated, the al-Atrash leadership had to deal with overthrow attempts in the Druze Mountain. The dilemma here was the medium strength of Ottoman power, which was strong enough to dismantle closed trust groups but less so to create property-holding imperial subjects directly attached to the state.

Two opposing trends emerged in the near frontier. Under the watchful eye of Abdulhamid II, there was relative tranquility in northern Iraq. The Sultan managed to keep the status quo in the region by consolidating *seyid* leaderships. Communal violence shaped the historical experience of eastern Anatolia. The region hosted Armenian peasants, Christian missionaries, Armenian revolutionaries, involuntary Muslim immigrants, tribal Kurdish leadership and non-Sunni Alevis. As such, it was the demographically-diverse and politically-divided character of the region that crystallized friend/foe distinctions and created alternative mobilizational networks on the ground.

Historically speaking, the Armenian nationalist movement challenged the status quo first in eastern Anatolia during the 1890s. Shielded with a social-democratic discourse, the revolutionaries campaigned for Armenian peasant rights and incited small-scale revolts across the region. The Ottoman response to revolutionary activity was two-fold. First, the central state cooperated with Sufi networks to build ideological hegemony. The *Nakşibendi-Khalidi* Sufi order received special recognition in this regard because of its strong mobilizing potential, pro-state approach, and anti-Christian stand.[56] Second, the Ottomans organized smaller tribes into Hamidiye cavalry regiments in order to fight the Armenian nationalist movement more effectively.[57]

The turning point for Muslim violence against the Armenians was the promise of domestic reform in six Ottoman provinces in the Berlin Congress (1878).[58] All sides interpreted the treaty as a pretext for foreign intervention.[59] Yet, similar to the situation in Macedonia, what made social conflict deadly was neither international pressure nor communal identities per se. The key was how communal identities were politicized and mobilized in an interactive fashion via Western missionary activity, *Nakşibendi* Sufi networks, Armenian nationalist propaganda, and Kurdish tribal regiments. This view even found strong support in the pages of the contemporary journal *Kurdistan* which was published by the most influential Kurdish dissident family in exile.[60]

Three patterns of contentious action characterized the frontier trajectory in the long run (Figure 2). In the far frontier, there were massive rebellions for local autonomy. As the Yemeni example shows, frontier elites were successful in their bargain with the central state. In the intermediate zone of lower Iraq and Hawran, where neither state nor local leaders fully controlled the situation, revolts of smaller scale targeted the local elite and the Ottoman state to regain customary rights. In the near frontier, relative tranquility was the norm. The Ottoman state was stronger and had similar interests and confessional affinity with local leaderships. What made eastern Anatolia a unique case was the mobilization of communal units by skillful brokers whose agendas were backed up by the Ottoman state and foreign powers on opposite sides.

Despite its ferocity and strength, Ottoman frontier mobilization was constrained on a number of accounts. The first reason has to do with the organizational nature of the insurgency. Religious brokers were effective short-term campaigners, yet were less successful in sustaining long term resistance movements. Moreover, building on fragile alliances, political coalitions in the frontier were always temporary and segmented in nature. While certain tribes, clans, and members of ruling households could oppose the state, others might side with the central authority. As such, collaboration with and resistance to the central state did not represent a fixed position in the Ottoman frontiers. The easy collapse of Kurdish opposition during the 1830s is an open testimony to this point.[61]

Second, in accordance with indirect-rule tradition, the Ottomans wisely rewarded the successful revolt leader in order to incorporate him into the imperial political machinery. Taxfarms, administrative positions, imperial stipends and political pardons were widely used strategies to include Yazidi, Yemeni, Rashidi, Saudi, Druze and Kurdish leaderships into the Ottoman framework. Furthermore, using rebellion as a bargaining tool, the rebel leader never wanted to let it get out of hand. Economic and political stakes were so high that there was almost always a local competitor around who would cooperate with the Ottoman state. As Andrew Gould states, frontier elites had no "ideological commitment to rebellion."[62]

The final element that checked frontier mobilization – at least in the near frontier – was the growing idea of territoriality, which limited the political opportunity space for tribal–rural

	OTTOMAN STATE STRENGTH*	IMMEDIACY OF FOREIGN INTERVENTION	CONFESSIONAL IDENTITY	COLLECTIVE ACTION OUTCOME
Eastern Anatolia	High	High	Similar	Communal Violence
Northern Iraq	High	Low	Similar	Stability
Hawran / Lower Iraq	Medium	Lower to Medium	Different	Small-Scale Revolts
Hijaz / Gulf Region	Low	Medium to High	Similar	Observing Status Quo
Yemen/Asir	Low	High	Different	Massive Rebellions

*In relative terms within the frontier trajectory

Figure 2   Collective Action in the Ottoman Frontier

unrest. This trend was perfectly demonstrated in the only, and unsuccessful, Kurdish revolt in eastern Anatolia (1879–1880) when a *Nakşibendi* leader with ideological influence and material interests on both sides of the border was contained through negotiations and political-exile strategy. The novel element was how the Iranian and Ottoman Empires could reach a temporary agreement to curb the power of a local leader whose influence threatened regional political stability and created international repercussions.[63]

Conclusions

There was thin rule in the frontier during the late Ottoman period. The Ottoman state operated with little institutionalization, relying on mutual cooperation, high trust, or coercive incorporation. Accordingly, there was no mass conscription, population census or land registration in places like the Arabian Peninsula. The politics of emergency sealed this vision when the central state realized the limits of its rule, the intensification of geopolitical rivalry, and the strength of local resistance in these regions. In fact, it was this inseparable trio that shaped the patterns of modern state-formation in Middle Eastern frontiers.

The existence of culturally distinct and politically autonomous groups of non-Sunni faith also gave a distinct character to Ottoman rule in the frontiers. Ideological challenges from the middle classes, merchants' economic priorities, and the political domination of an urban Muslim bloc did not materialize, making it harder for the Ottoman state to penetrate the frontier society. Unable to connect with the local elite or transform the region with imperial institutions (or through an aggressive settler policy), the Ottomans put the emphasis on a moral agenda. Yet, the confessional Sunni agenda of the imperial state also backfired especially in the far frontiers, and turned eastern Anatolia into a more contentious zone during the 1890s.

The power of religious and rural leaderships also influenced the economic options available in the region. Protection-money collection and the subsistence economy remained as the major sources of income, followed by tax-farming, smuggling, and the slave trade. It was only in the near frontier, where state centralization was relatively stronger and urban interests cooperated with the central state, that regional markets flourished. Transjordan and northern Iraq were two such regional examples. Nonetheless, tax-farming still enjoyed an undisputed leadership position. It is worth remembering that 80 percent of land in lower Iraq still technically belonged to the central state in 1914.

Collective action in the frontier was motivated by local autonomy perspectives against a centralizing Ottoman state. Frontier resistance was rurally-based, benefited from heterodox brands of Islam, and was most rewarding when there were religious actors on the ground to unite the frontier elites. As such, it was the relationship between gatekeeper frontier elites and itinerant religious brokers that determined the degree of success in the frontiers.[64] While their merger under a single authority sustained long-term rebellions in the far frontiers the separation of the two sparked short-term tribal revolts and anti-landlord discourse in lower Iraq, south-eastern Anatolia, and Druze Mountain. Yet their cooperation created another historical outcome: social upheavals with a communal character in eastern Anatolia.

As a final note, it is worth mentioning that collective claims in the Ottoman frontiers asked for better bargains from the central state. Frontier leaders neither fully detached themselves from imperial authority in Istanbul nor pursued deliberate policies for political independence. As the Treaty of Da'an with Imam Yahya and the agreement of al-Hafair with Idrisi attest, even far frontier leaders were content with the idea of some kind of hereditary rule arrangement within the Ottoman framework. It is safe to argue that this situation continued until the dark days of World War despite the intensity of protest, high frequency of revolts, and widespread character of resistance.

Having introduced the coast, interior and frontier as regional paths during the nineteenth century, the next chapter turns to the closing days of the Ottoman Empire and discusses how imperial trajectories underwent a drastic revision with the Young Turk Revolution, mass politics and major wars between 1908 and 1922.

CHAPTER 5

ROUTES OF TRANSFORMATION, 1908–1922

The 1908–1922 was a new epoch in late Ottoman history. Mass politics allowed social actors to sraise novel demands, and major wars paved the way for the dissolution of the Ottoman Empire. Rapid political transformation also revised imperial trajectories. Mass politics pitted local actors against the new imperial class, the point of contention being the distinct identity of each regional path. Accordingly, frontier leaderships insisted on local autonomy, coastal middle classes raised issues of imperial reform and economic integration, and the Muslim bloc tried to protect its intermediary position in inland regions. The war episode resolved these domestic disputes in different ways. It changed internal hierarchies on the coast, discontinued the interior path, and sealed the distinct character of the Ottoman frontier.

This chapter examines routes of transformation in the late Ottoman Empire. The first section surveys the rise of the new imperial class, who came up with an agenda of change during the Second Constitutional Period. The second section traces the victory of nationalism on the coast and shows how communal hinterlands and nationalist middle classes prevailed over cosmopolitan others. In the third section, my goal is to draw attention to the failed bargains in the interior, where Muslim rule came under pressure with Ottoman collapse. The final section suggests that the war episode consolidated predatory regimes in the Arabian Peninsula, yet weakened politically autonomous communities in the rest of the frontier.

The New Imperial Class

Multiplying from 2,000 scribal servants to 35,000 bureaucrats in the Abdulhamidian era, the modern bureaucracy in the Ottoman Empire was a late Ottoman reality.[1] It emerged as a response to outside military pressure, acquired a reformist character in the process, and gave birth to a distinct social class by the turn of the twentieth century. The long-term impact of the bureaucratic groups is remarkable: they altered state–society relations throughout the empire, and shaped several political outcomes in the post-Ottoman Balkans and the modern Middle East. Ottoman bureaucracy evolved in three distinct phases.

The first phase (1787–1839) was about neutralizing the rival groups in the political scene. Military defeats by imperial Russia, and the uncontested power of ayans, convinced the Ottoman rulers to upgrade war-making capabilities and start a process of centralization. Selim III set up a small modern army and opened up schools of higher learning in military science and medicine.[2] His successor, Mahmut II, destroyed the once powerful janissary groups and constrained the autonomy of governors and local rulers in Anatolia and the Balkans. As of 1830, Ottoman military reorganization successfully eliminated vested-interest groups in the capital and weakened the local elite in the provinces. In doing so, it cleared the way for new institution-building and terminated the organizational bases of autonomous leaderships.

The crushing victories of Muhammad Ali of Egypt forced the Ottoman Sultan to extend reforms beyond the military realm. The great reforms of the Tanzimat promised equal rights to non-Muslims, made the legal framework compatible with the needs of the capitalist world economy, and introduced several regulations for an efficient provincial administration.[3] As such, the second phase of bureaucratic transformation (1839–1875) was characterized by the hegemonic idea of reform and several novel institutions. The Ottomans needed European support for political survival, yet pursued centralization policies to prevent further territorial losses. The major problem from the Ottoman perspective at this time was the limited number of trained bureaucrats to implement reforms, especially in the provinces.

In the age of imperialism, the Ottoman state concentrated its efforts on training more professionals for imperial bureaucracy and formulating defensive ideologies for political survival. In this respect, the domestic agenda behind the pan-Islamic policy of Abdulhamid II was to achieve imperial cohesion via institutional and moral means. The former strategy meant improving the empire's infrastructure in public education and soon brought Ottoman bureaucratic rule to its maturity. Accordingly, the third phase of bureaucratic consolidation (1876–1908) was

The new imperial class and positivism. Medical School (Tıbbiye Mektebi) students.

characterized by the "thickening of administrative posture", and created a new imperial class whose self-assigned mission was to protect the territorial integrity of the Ottoman Empire.[4]

The new imperial class was multi-lingual, multi-ethnic, and predominantly Muslim. Modern education gave them distinct qualities such as professionalism and elitism that set them apart from religious and propertied classes in the empire.[5] They believed in the idea of top-down reform, distrusted local leaderships and foreign powers, and distanced themselves from the autocratic policies of the Sultan. Their effective use of journalism abroad, easy access to bureaucratic power, and secretive underground organizations made the Young Turk opposition a credible threat. At this point, the agreement between Russia and Britain about the political future of Macedonia convinced the discontented members of the bureaucratic class that foreign intervention to the Ottoman Empire was imminent.

Credit for overthrowing the autocratic regime belonged to the Salonica wing of the opposition, that united junior military officers stationed in Macedonia with intellectuals positioned in the provincial bureaucracy. Macedonia played a prominent role in the proclamation of the constitution for several reasons. First, the Macedonian hinterland showed the military officers the fragile nature of Ottoman rule in the frontiers. Second, the port-city of Salonica with its receptive Jewish economic elite, politically influential Muslim landlord class, and powerful *dönme* families provided the necessary political opportunity space for the opposition to get organized. Finally, the insurgent movements operating in the region taught Ottoman officers new tactics of dissent to make their case for an Ottoman constitution.[6]

Refusing to obey military orders, a small group of rebel army officers took refuge in the mountains, leaving the Sultan no choice but to resume the Constitution on July 23, 1908. Controlling the forces of opposition in Salonica, the Committee of Union and Progress (CUP) built their case on two key premises to run the Ottoman Empire. While unity would erase the differences among *millets* and transform them into citizens with a supranational

Ottomanist identity (*ittihad-ı anasır*), the notion of progress would create a modern Ottoman state along European lines. The expectation of the CUP leadership was that the reformist agenda would put the Ottoman Empire into a respectable position in the international arena and arrest the secessionist movements inside imperial borders.

The CUP introduced several proposals to implement far-reaching reforms in the Ottoman Empire. These included a non-confessional political system that would eliminate quotas for religious groups, professionalism in bureaucratic service that would replace the politically networked individuals with efficient administrators on the spot, and a notion of equality that would promote the idea of a truly multi-religious empire. Hence, the success of the CUP program then hinged upon the elimination of intermediary groups. It was believed that fast-track social change from above would turn the "Sick man of Europe" into the "Japan of the Near East" and create a politically independent, militarily strong, and economically rich Ottoman Empire.[7]

Projecting an Ottoman identity. Religious leaders and imperial elite at the ballot-box.

To the surprise of the CUP leadership, the centralization agenda of the Young Turks faced major setbacks in the international arena and on the home front.[8] A few weeks after the proclamation of the Constitution, Austria annexed Bosnia–Herzegovina, Crete became part of Greece, and Bulgaria declared its independence from the Ottoman Empire. On the home front, there was no agreement with the revolutionary movements in the Balkans and eastern Anatolia, disturbances occurred in the frontier regions such as Hawran and Transjordan, and the Muslim bloc as well as the Greek Orthodox Church resented the centralization attempts of the Istanbul government that would trim their intermediary powers.

The lame position of the CUP became clear with the parliamentary elections of 1908. The elections aptly demonstrated the provincial bias in politics throughout the empire. Aykut Kansu claims that only 15 percent of members of the parliament (44/281) were affiliated with the CUP.[9] Following the elections, there was a counter-revolution attempt in the capital and the liberal–decentralist opposition consolidated in the parliament. Campaigning from an anti-CUP platform, the latter raised local concerns and criticized the Committee's stand on Turkification and Islam.[10] Still, the opposition did not deliver political results. Liberal Entente failed to create an alliance with the Greek Orthodox Church and non-Turkish parliamentarians, hardly existed outside the capital as a political organization, and faced the vengeance of CUP at the polls in 1912.[11]

Intra-elite competition and "center–periphery" tensions took new turns when mass politics (1908–1918) and the war episode (1912–1922) transformed the political experience of the Ottoman Empire. Each imperial trajectory was now subject to major revision. The story of the Ottoman coast proved to be no different. In less than a decade, the bright future of the port-city faded from the horizon and was replaced by a nightmare scenario in which cosmopolitan peace was sacrificed for the greater good of political irredentism, nation-state building, and colonial greed.

Nationalizing the Coast

The Ottoman coast was enthusiastic about the Young Turk Revolution. A wave of worker demonstrations, strikes and socialist agitation soon politicized the port-city.[12] Workers demanded more rights in Salonica, Izmir and Beirut, and challenged the privileged position of international and domestic capital. Middle classes also got organized. This was especially true in Beirut where a compact urban elite asked for more representative and efficient institutions to develop the province from the bottom up and keep it competitive on the world economic stage.[13] The Committee's response to coastal interests was less than cooperative. The government banned worker demonstrations as a law-and-order problem, and resented the middle classes with tougher regulations on the associational realm.

Subsequently, the CUP began to search for new political allies on the Ottoman coast. Economic boycotts reflected this state of mind, and increasingly challenged the hegemonic presence of cosmopolitan classes. The main target of post-1909 boycotts was Ottoman Greeks. They were accused of supporting the Greek army during the Balkan Wars through material donations. At this critical moment, the government decided to disrupt non-Muslim commercial interests in the port-city and turned to Muslim and Jewish guild workers for help.[14] This was a wise choice. The latter group enjoyed an almost complete monopoly over port operations and could easily hurt economic interests connected to foreign trade.

The other CUP strategy to keep the port-city in check was geared towards the hinterland. This was most visible in western Anatolia, where political intervention in favor of Muslim landlords strengthened local producers by challenging the monopoly of European and non-Muslim merchants over price and credit. Likewise, in Mount Lebanon and Jabal Amil, the Committee bypassed the Maronite majority and worked with Druze and Shiite leaderships. The new political framework soon created strong leaders (*za'ims*) in the countryside who could mobilize locally and still think in imperial terms. The best known member of this group was the Druze Amir Shakib Arslan. A firm believer in the unity of the empire, he served the Ottoman state in several capacities.[15]

Starting with the Balkan Wars, homogenization of the coastal space became a bold ambition in the eastern Mediterranean. Political change came with military intervention, and consolidated through economic, political and demographic means. First, the Greek state doubled its territory with the Balkan Wars, capturing most of Macedonia. The subsequent Muslim emigration and the Great Fire of 1917 made Salonica more Greek.[16] In Lebanon, the French colonial project empowered the Maronite community of Mount Lebanon by attaching cosmopolitan Beirut to the new state of Greater Lebanon. In western Anatolia, the CUP annulled the capitulations during the Great War and implemented several measures to promote Muslim interests.

The latter development in particular was linked to the collapse of foreign trade with war, and ignited economic nationalism in (western) Anatolia. Accordingly, the share of mills in industrial production increased from 32 percent in 1913 to 44 percent in 1915.[17] Even then, production levels were lagging behind consumption, causing food shortages in urban areas. In the capital city, the CUP established strong connections with former guilds (*esnaf cemiyetleri*[18]), and mobilized Anatolian merchants to participate in national companies that were set up to meet the provisioning needs of Istanbul.[19] In a short span of time, war economy not only hurt non-Muslim merchants, but also consolidated Muslim interests on the outskirts of the coastal hinterland and in central Anatolia.

Still, the major port-cities of the Ottoman Empire were under Christian rule in 1920. Belligerent states revised the political realities in favor of local Christians, making the CUP intervention in western Anatolia a war-time anomaly. Greeks in Izmir and the Maronites in Greater Lebanon were celebrating the dawn of a new era as they returned home to western Anatolia after the Great War and migrated to Beirut from the Mountain. Like the Lyon Chamber of Commerce, European and domestic actors alike believed that the belle époque of the Ottoman port-city could be recovered under "enlightened" leaderships, and the economic integration of the Ottoman coast to world markets could be resumed.

Their optimistic view proved to be partially accurate. The defeat of Greek forces at the hands of the Turkish resistance movement reversed the political process in western Anatolia. Earlier Turkish success stemmed from local organizing at the outskirts of the hinterland, where there was established Muslim leadership and integration to world markets remained weaker and qualitatively different.[20] In Lebanon, the same strategy could not be replicated. Muslims in the port-towns of Sidon and Tripoli refused to participate in the Maronite-dominated French system, yet lacked a class of brokers to link up with Druze and Shiite discontent in southern Lebanon and the Beqaa Valley.[21] That class of brokers was the imperial class in Anatolia who first coordinated the resistance movement in different regions and later gave it a national character.

When the dust finally settled on the eastern Mediterranean, coastal experience looked quite different. Most importantly, nationalist and colonial projects broke up the Ottoman framework and homogenized the coast via population transfers and warmaking.[22] In Lebanon, where this was partially not an option, the solution was to set up a confessional system and give Muslims and Christians communal representation with unequal shares. In all of the cases above, communal hinterlands benefited from this abrupt transformation and penetrated the rich and powerful port-city which was once reserved for urban and cosmopolitan groups. Still, the port-city middle classes from the winning camp managed to stay on top, embracing the new political authority and mobilizing their energies for the national good and/or colonial interest.[23]

If the triumph of nationalism brought a speedy conclusion to hostilities on the Ottoman coast, the struggle in the interior was just beginning. The fall of Abdulhamid and the collapse of the Ottoman Empire would turn the world upside down for the interior regimes and eventually bring them down in Syria and Palestine.

Failed Bargains in the Interior

Inland towns were unmoved by the Revolution of 1908. As the main beneficiaries of the absolutist Abdulhamidian era, members of the Muslim bloc were concerned about the uncertain future of electoral politics and shared deep suspicions about CUP rule. Their fears soon became true. Purges in the bureaucracy eliminated provincial posts, discourse on religious equality undermined Muslim supremacy, and centralization measures promised to undercut the mediating functions of local notables. Gathered around the Muhammadan Union, the local *ulema* of central Anatolia and Damascus struck back. They promised to make sharia supreme throughout the empire and prevent secular measures from taking root in the Ottoman legal system.

Soon after, a more effective opposition developed in Syria. Using electoral politics and constitutional freedoms, Arabists raised novel demands to strike a new political bargain with the central state. A key member of this group, Shukri Asali, asked for a larger share for Arabs in the bureaucracy and turned the attention of the Ottoman public to Zionism as a major threat in Palestine.[24] This proactive position was also evident throughout the debates surrounding language policy. The Arabists insisted on the use of Arabic in public institutions despite the fact that Young Turk policy was consistent with the previous Abdulhamidian practice.[25] In this respect, Arabism was neither a movement towards Arab independence nor a reaction to "Turkification" policies.[26] It was rather a genuine attempt by a small group of activists who made new claims from the central state.

The Arabist movement had discrete origins. Political leadership came from the discontented members of the Muslim bloc who lost public office after 1908 and engaged in middle-class professions. Its ideological repertoire derived from the secular discourse of cultural nationalism, yet included elements from the Islamic-modernism thesis of Muhammad Abduh and Rashid Rida in Egypt. In organizational terms, the Young Arab Society (Fatat) and Covenant Society (Ahd) were founded by Syrian and Iraqi members of the imperial class who envisioned radical change from above. Despite its exponential impact with mass politics, Arabism remained a minority position in the Arab world before World War I.[27]

The Great War demonstrated why this was historically the case. First and foremost, the Committee emphasized Muslim solidarity as the basis of Ottoman Empire after the loss of Balkan territories, and promoted an Islamic version of Ottomanism to keep its Arab provinces intact. In line with this perspective, they accepted some of the Arabist demands and were able to get many influential Arabists back into the political process in 1914.[28] Second, the Muslim bloc realized that the inexperienced revolutionaries in the capital were willing to share power in the provinces despite their progressive discourse and vocal anti-localism. Finally, for the Arab public at large, the war represented a clash between a legitimate Islamic empire and an imperialist West. This perception generated widespread support for the Ottomans even in Egypt, which was then under British occupation.

War also brought unprecedented misery to inland regions. As war lingered on, the Ottoman Empire had great difficulty in financing the war effort, finding new recruits for war mobilization, and dealing with social and economic problems. Before anything else, this had to do with the structural weaknesses of the Ottoman state.[29] The Ottoman Empire was a low-capacity state and was the least prepared of all warring parties. Short-sighted policy and poor individual decisions also contributed to political instability in the interior. Syria figured as a low priority provisioning zone in the Committee's list, war mobilization (*seferberlik*) destroyed life as usual in Palestine, and Cemal Paşa viewed Arabists as "traitors" and hanged them in Damascus.[30] The cumulative impact of war was to increase local discontent in the Arab provinces and tilt the balance towards non-Ottoman solutions.[31]

Major economic changes took place with war in the interior. Most strikingly, Muslim merchants benefited from national-economy policies in central Anatolia. The grain corridor that stretched from Kayseri to Adapazarı shipped no less than 3,600 freight cars of foodtuffs to Istanbul, where prices skyrocketed in less than three years. An unprecendented wave of inflation and speculation turned into nice profits for the interior merchants who invested their capital into joint-stock companies and strengthened their political ties with the Committee. The Arab interior had a different experience. Regional economic ties were shattered under war conditions and disconnected Syria from Anatolia, Palestine and Lebanon. Aleppo province in particular emerged as a direct loser from the war, and lost its important economic partners in Anatolia and northern Iraq.

When the war was over in 1918, Arabists prevailed over the Ottomanists in the Arab world. The Ottoman Empire was gone and the armies of Faysal and the British arrived in Damascus the same year. The new political framework promised to represent Arab rights and create a territorial state along the same lines. Arab nationalism then became the "right ideology" to make a political claim and access governmental power. Its most powerful brand was pan-Arabism. The pan-Arabist movement was dominated by the imperial-Arab elite who had been brought up in the Ottoman framework. While Iraqi recruits were men of modest means educated in military schools, Syrians and Palestinians came from the civil-bureaucracy tradition.[32] All dreamed of an expanded Arab state that united the former Arab provinces of the Ottoman Empire.

Meanwhile, the Muslim bloc experienced an "express conversion" to Arab nationalism after the war. Their future still looked

War mobilization. Recruiting for the army near Tiberias, 1914.

Ottoman army. Ottoman soldiers' daily ration in Palestine, 1917.

bleak. The chaotic regime of Faysal (1918–1920) distributed resources at will, ignored members of the Muslim bloc, and lacked a capacity to enforce law and order in the region. Their piecemeal demands and localism also put them at odds with pan-Arabists whose political idealism and "transnational" goals were perhaps matched only by their failed pan-Turkist counterparts in Asia.[33] Finally, the majority had a reason to believe in localist solutions. They owned resources and controlled cultural frames in Syria and Palestine and did not want to share them with "tribal" Hijazis and military (*askeri*) groups from Iraq.

The Clamanceau–Faysal Agreement ended the pan-Arabist dream in 1920. What this meant for Syria and Palestine was not only the establishment of colonial rule but also the re-emergence of the localist position under a new political discourse. In Palestine, with the shattering of the Greater Syria idea and the rising number of Jews, Palestinian identity began to grow. In the Syrian province, local committees were set up to defend the homeland against French invasion.[34] The most spectacular resistance to French rule took place in the province of Aleppo, where a former Ottoman officer, Ibrahim Hananu harrassed the French army for two years in close cooperation with Turkish nationalists who were then fighting in the north of the same province.[35]

The Syrian resistance (1919–1921) showed the real sources of power in the Ottoman interior, and gave a snapshot of the identity crisis that was taking place in the region after Ottoman retreat. As in inland western Anatolia, local resistance proved the leadership qualities and organizational skills of the Muslim bloc, who mobilized the common folk by utilizing horizontal ties and circumventing vertical hierarchies. The resistance also demonstrated that the underlying rationale for defense in the Arab interior was not exclusively tied to nationalism, but also stemmed from local, regional and imperial concerns. This was most visible in Aleppo province, whose political future, economic orientation, and rivalry with Damascus remained unsolved for years to come.

With the defeat of the Syrian resistance in 1921, a new power struggle unfolded in the Ottoman interior. Most importantly, the French mandate tried to find new political partners in the "Levant". For this purpose, several minority groups were given separate administrations (Alawites, Druze), and rural Muslims from less-established backgrounds were recruited to the Levant army. In Palestine, the demographic expansion of Jews and the British presence in the region put the local leaderships of Palestine into a difficult position. Land purchases in particular put the communal solidarity of Arab residents at risk, yet contributed to a growing local-resistance movement against Jewish settlements.

In sum, the Arab interior experienced dramatic political change during the 1908–1922 period. The failed bargains between minority Arabists and the Ottoman state destroyed the half-century old status quo in these regions. In the aftermath of the Great War, the Muslim bloc was forced to fight an uphill battle to regain its monopoly over political space. Fellow Arab states, mandate authorities, religious minorities, Jews in Palestine, and pan-Arabists were now new political actors that had to be taken into account.

Making Frontiers Independent

The Young Turk era started with the Armenian Question in the frontiers. The revolutionaries asked for comprehensive decentralization measures for eastern Anatolia and proposed a land reform to end the plight of Armenian peasants. In this respect, the Armenian demands were to institutionalize local autonomy along ethnic lines and to implement egalitarian land and taxation policies in the region. By promoting an economic program, the Armenian platform also departed from pre-war Muslim nationalisms and found sympathetic ears in CUP circles. Still, the Armenian plea for autonomy failed. The government viewed centralization as the only remedy to change the status quo in eastern Anatolia and opposed any political move towards decentralization.[36]

Autonomy demands stood a better chance in the intermediate zones of lower Iraq and southern Syria. Tribes successfully rebelled in the least integrated *sancak* of Transjordan, destroying everything Ottoman.[37] Their main target was state centralization that brought not only soldiers, but also grain merchants, the Hijaz Railway, and Ottoman Islam to the region. Meanwhile, the expanding British patronage networks in the Gulf area forced the influential leader of Basra, Sayyid Talip to seek autonomy. Using modern political means, he campaigned for imperial decentralization. With this strategic move, Talip's main idea was to balance his position vis-à-vis Kuwaiti leadership and keep his options open while negotiating with the Ottomans and the British.

The real change, though, came in the far frontier, where the Ottoman state was forced to grant regional autonomy to local leaderships. This was a novel development for two reasons. Most importantly, for the first time, the Ottomans acknowledged in writing the sovereign status of frontier leaderships. The central state gave them hereditary titles, or at least accepted the right of frontier leaderships to collect taxes and administer justice. Second, these unusal measures came under extraordinary conditions. Frontier leaders used an ongoing imperial (defensive) war as a political opportunity to start a rebellion and get their demands on the table. Accordingly, it was the Italo–Ottoman and the subsequent Balkan Wars that secured legal autonomy for northern Yemen, Asir and Najd.

There was, however, one exception to this rule before 1914. While the rest of the Arabian Peninsula was able to strike a new deal with the central state, the Sharif of Mecca was busy trying to block the centralization attempts of the Istanbul government.[38] The Ottoman state made it clear that his services were no more needed in Medina and his "mini-government" in Mecca had to be dismantled. After the Hijaz Railroad reached Medina in 1908, Sharif viewed railroad connection to Mecca as political suicide and refused to cooperate with the central state. At this point, the Great War gave Sharif Husayn of Mecca a once-in-a-life-time opportunity to turn the tide. With British material subsidies and military support, he could easily beat back the Ottomans and his regional rivals and establish a territorially expanded Arab kingdom.[39]

The "Arab Revolt" during the Great War then was primarily about changing regional balances in the Peninsula. With no Arab nationalism in the air, first, Saudi and Hijazi forces clashed in a major conflict. Soon after, other regional actors also joined the British camp to eliminate their archrivals and complicated the situation in the Peninsula. Touted by the British government of India, Saud occupied a strategic position in the region. His main opponent was the pro-Ottoman Rashidi leadership who controlled access to northern Arabia as well as a vibrant smuggling network to Kuwait. The Saudis also established a valuable partnership with Idrisi of Asir. The latter was under pressure from north and south, and could have easily fallen prey to the expansionist scheme of Sharif Husayn of Mecca or Imam Yahya of Yemen.

Call for Jihad. Sharif of Medina supporting the Ottoman war effort in Medina, 1914.

During the war years, the Ottoman Empire persisted in the near frontier. In contrast to the imperial experience on the Arabian Peninsula, the Ottomans had stronger local allies in eastern Anatolia and faced only a short-lived military intervention to the region. A major demographic change during the war also favored the Ottoman cause: Armenians were forcefully deported and transferred to Syria for security reasons.[40] As such, the political recipe that kept eastern Anatolia Ottoman was three-fold: (1) the expulsion of Armenians en masse, (2) the active support of the Muslim community for a pro-Ottoman solution, and (3) the earlier withdrawal of the Russian army from the War. Not surprisingly, then, the only part of the frontier left in Ottoman hands in 1919 was eastern Anatolia.

The political struggle over the near frontier continued after the war. The victorious Allies promised to establish Armenian and Kurdish states in eastern Anatolia with the Treaty of Sèvres. Subsequently, both nationalisms posed a serious challenge to the growing Turkish resistance movement in 1919–1922. The Armenian option was eliminated after a military victory in Gümrü and the follow-up Kars Treaty that secured the borders in the Caucasus. The Kurdish demands were more difficult to deal with. The Kurdish elite was part of the political establishment, the religious leaderships received state support for promoting Ottoman unity against Armenian nationalist activity, and the Islamic community in the region had lived under Ottoman rule for centuries.

In this critical juncture, the divided nature of Kurdish opposition helped the Turkish cause. Kurdish nationalism was promoted by the educated and younger generations of frontier elites who spent most of their lives in Istanbul or abroad. The most influential member of this group was the Bedirhan family. After the war, a number of locally powerful bureaucratic families also switched their allegiance to nationalism and promoted the Kurdish cause.[41] Still, powerful religious figures on the spot disagreed with the nationalists' plea for independence and favored the idea of autonomy for eastern Anatolia.[42]

The political experience of frontier societies diverged after Ottoman collapse. Nationalist administrations prevailed in the near frontier. Turkish nationalists marginalized the Kurdish opposition and crushed its Islamic variant with force.[43] In northern Iraq, local Kurdish leadership lost its bargaining ground when the League of Nations granted the Mosul province to Iraq in 1926, and the British mandate rule approved the centralist vision of Sunni officers in Baghdad. In the intermediate zone, mandate authorities consolidated landlord *şeyhs* in lower Iraq, and encouraged clans to challenge the political monopoly of al-Atrash leadership on Druze Mountain.[44] In the far frontier, the Saudi state terminated the material base and political autonomy of Rashidi, Hijazi and al-Ahsa leaderships, and destroyed *Ikhwan*, the fighting force that once guaranteed territorial expansion and served the religious cause of Wahhabism.[45]

The 1908–1922 period was most beneficial to frontier leaderships. They successfully secured local autonomy, defeated centralization policies, and later got rid of Ottoman rule with World War I. Political energies were then spent on regional political consolidation especially in the Arabian Peninsula. Around the same time, institutionalizing autonomy or acquiring independence became harder to achieve in the rest of the frontier. The Ottoman state was relatively powerful in the near frontier, and the European colonizers had high stakes in the intermediate zone. Accordingly, eastern Anatolia, northern Iraq and southern Syria continued to resist mandate rule and/or national authorities in order to retain or regain autonomy during the 1920s.

Conclusions

The three imperial trajectories went through a dramatic revision during the 1908–1922 period. First, mass politics shook the internal hierarchies throughout the empire. The economic redistribution agenda of workers in the port-cities, the political demands of the new imperial class in the Arab provinces, and local autonomy movements in the frontiers demonstrated that the status quo in each path was now subject to internal pressure. Still, it was the war episode that created national coasts, mandates in the interior, and independent frontiers. It is also worth mentioning that the Ottoman collapse was initiated by the most threatened actor (Sharif of Mecca) of the least integrated trajectory (frontier) and worked best for the most distant actor (Saud of Najd) in the imperial universe.

More broadly put, there were winners and losers from this dramatic transformation. By becoming politically independent and keeping regional structures intact, religious trust networks of the far frontier benefited the most from Ottoman collapse. In the rest of the frontier, local leaderships faced the vengeance of modern states. Meanwhile, communal hinterlands and nationalist middle classes prevailed over cosmopolitan elements on the Ottoman coast and turned the Muslims of Greece and Christians of western Anatolia into "political liabilities". The Arab interior received the heaviest blow from Ottoman collapse. The urban Muslim bloc lost regional markets with imperial partition and faced several political challenges that came from domestic competitors and mandate authorities.

The most dramatic impact of imperial trajectories on post-Ottoman reality was on state formation. Each modern state now possessed a political territory that bundled different Ottoman trajectories under the same framework. The eclectic character of newly founded Middle Eastern states made national integration impossible in the region. In this respect, the most important Ottoman legacy for the Middle East in the interwar period was the resilience of regional paths where locally embedded social networks continued to promote rival programs concerning state–society and local–global relations in each state.

CONCLUSION

Using a path-dependent framework, this book has argued that the Ottoman Middle East was characterized by three regional trajectories during the nineteenth century. These were the coast, the interior and the frontier. Regional paths were rival social orders that came to represent distinct routes to modernity in the region. Accordingly, the coastal experience was shaped by global flows, inland regions evolved with Ottoman state-building effort, and the frontiers kept their autonomy from the central state and modernization processes. The key was the alternative institutionalization of economy, politics and collective claims that secured the hegemony of different social networks in each regioal path.

In the conclusion, my goal is to draw further attention to the advantages of the trajectory idea. I start off by providing a short summary of the book, emphasizing its key points. Then, I show how the idea of regional paths can lead to fresh interpretations and new findings in Ottoman and Middle Eastern history. Finally, I raise comparative research questions to "make the trajectory framework work" in late Ottoman and Middle Eastern Studies.

Late Ottoman Trajectories

I began this book by noting that late Ottoman historiography has been characterized by mono-causal approaches and propensity accounts since World War II. The former credited capitalism or Westernization as the only dynamic that transformed the late

Ottoman experience during the nineteenth century. Recently, the latter has emphasized the political bargains between local actors and the Ottoman state, and reintroduced center–periphery models. Despite their valuable contributions to the field, structural and agency explanations have major shortcomings. Most importantly, they fail to come up with an intra-Ottoman perspective and lack an analytical template to explain the different constitutive roles played by the Ottoman state, global processes and local actors at the same time.

This project has put forward a novel framework for understanding the late Ottoman Middle East during the nineteenth century. Departing from modernization approaches, macro models and bargaining perspectives, I have argued that the regional trajectory framework is a better analytical tool and empirical strategy. It is spatial, path-dependent and comparative. The framework is attentive to local dynamics, prioritizes regional time over imperial time, and views the Middle East in terms of variation. As such, it explains the great divergence in the Ottoman Middle East with reference to variation over the same processes. Furthermore, its emphasis on sequence makes it an interactive analysis, and accounts for changing relations between different parts of the empire.

The book introduced the coast, the interior and the frontier as competing regional experiences in the Ottoman Empire. Chapter 2 traced the evolution of middle-class rule on the Ottoman coast in relation to the global economy and emphasized the centrality of domestic non-Muslim merchants in the process. It also underlined the fact that the unique identity of the Ottoman coast consolidated under two historical conditions: (1) new economic wealth sponsored the rise of a public sphere that reflected the priorities of urban groups, and (2) collective claims in the eastern Mediterranean became a function of world economic integration.

My presentation of the interior trajectory in Chapter 3 demonstrated that a centralizing Ottoman state played a pivotal role in inland regions after 1860. The provincial bureaucracy was both the key mechanism and main point of contention for acquiring land deals, political posts and moral authority in inland regions. This only became possible when the Ottomans sealed off the region from foreign threat, the urban Muslim bloc believed in the Ottoman model, and institutional refinement in the Abdulhamidian era created a new layer of legitimacy for the Ottoman state. As such, the interior trajectory not only served the interests of powerful intermediaries, but also created powerful cultural frames and new institutional sites to sustain imperial rule.

In Chapter 4, I made the case that there was thin rule in the Ottoman frontiers. Local leaderships controlled economic resources, preserved heterodox cultural schemas, and organized collective resistance. When the Ottomans were unable to develop successful modern state-building in the frontiers, contentious collective action turned into an effective bargaining strategy. Comprising the largest mass mobilization effort in the region, revolts were rural in nature, relied on the brokerage skills of the religious entrepreneurs, and mobilized frontier Islam as an ideological frame. The goal was to protect local autonomy against a centralizing Ottoman state.[1]

The imperial paths examined throughout the book were revised in multiple ways from 1908 to 1922. Chapter 5 showed that this was mainly the outcome of large-scale territorial wars. Hence, the political success of nationalist and colonial projects (with World War I) guaranteed the great transformation of the region. It revised the coastal model in favor of hinterland interests and nationalist elites, weakened the Muslim bloc and regional markets in the interior, and cut off the frontiers from the Ottoman framework. In this respect, nation-building efforts on the coast, mandate rule in the interior, and new political regimes in the frontier represented historic moments in the life-cycle of each Ottoman path.

The late Ottoman world was still in existence during the 1920s. The coast sustained its global economic orientation, the new interior regimes were forced to recognize the power of the urban Muslim bloc, and the frontier was characterized by contentious collective action that aimed at local autonomy. The fate of Ottoman trajectories was sealed forever a decade later when global developments turned off the primary process that sustained the distinct character of each regional path. Accordingly, regional trajectories were finally terminated with the Great Depression, the rise of nation states, and the onset of cold war, as these historical trends severed global ties, weakened local Muslim coalitions, and terminated collective action in the frontiers respectively.

What about trajectory legacies? The collapse of the Ottoman Empire hurt the inland regimes of Syria and Palestine the most, as it opened these regions to foreign intervention and took away the organizational bases of the Muslim bloc's authority in the long run.[2] In contrast, as organizational analysis would predict, path-dependency was most visible in the frontier. The language of autonomy and/or the power of communal trust networks remained strong from eastern Anatolia to Yemen. Without its cosmopolitan cover and global markets, the coast took a nationalist turn. Not surprisingly, the modernizing project made its biggest impact on the coast of the eastern Mediterranean during the twentieth century.

Ottoman Insights

The trajectory idea provides new ways to rethink turning points, key processes and major outcomes in the Ottoman Empire and beyond. This study offers three comparative conclusions about frontiers. First, frontiers and borderlands were two different things in the late Ottoman Empire.[3] Frontiers were places where the power of the central state remained weak compared to existing practices in the rest of the empire. The Ottomans failed in the frontiers especially when they lacked cooperative local agents and/or operated in a less favorable international environment. In contrast, as the example of Greek–Ottoman border showed, borderlands could turn into managed spaces over time. Thus, while most Ottoman borderlands were frontiers, not all frontiers were borderlands.

Second, the Ottoman frontier was primarily a nineteenth-century reality. This was primarily the case because the frontier is a relational concept. It is meaningful as an analytical category only when its opposite pair(s) exists. Accordingly, the Ottoman frontier became a historical path in relation to coastal and interior regimes. It is also worth noting that the political rise of frontiers was also helped by the collapse of hegemonic world order. Global flows and multipolarity weakened Ottoman authority and Britain respectively, and turned the frontiers into contentious zones in the age of imperialism. This trend was visible in other contiguous empires as well.[4]

Third, frontier societies in the Middle East used their coercive skills for imperial mobility. Ottomans, the French and the British relied on highland societies such as Kurds, Albanians, Circassians, Alawites and Assyrians for (select) protection services in the region.[5] The rationale for recruiting these groups went beyond an ideological commitment to "martial-races theory". The key was trust. As closed networks, they were internally cohesive, yet had limited contacts with the larger society. In that respect, they were modern Mamluks who helped to solve the principal–agent problems of the ruler at several levels. From a reverse angle, this strategy also paid off. Iraqi-Sunni officers came close to usurping political power in mandate Iraq whereas Alawites later used the army to "hijack" the state in Syria.

The sociological evolution of the interior trajectory provides new ground to interpret Arab nationalism. As suggested earlier, Arab nationalism was neither a response to centralization nor a dedicated movement towards independence. Instead, the rise of an Arab imperial class showed the Ottoman institutional success in the interior. Having transformed themselves from provincial intermediaries to imperial bureaucrats, the new members of the ruling class tried to change imperial hierarchy in their own vision. They formulated new demands to diversify the Ottoman elite and to upgrade the political partnership between the Arab Muslim bloc and the imperial capital. It is worth noting that this became possible only when the imperial capital became an agent of change with the Young Turk Revolution.[6]

The rise of Arab elites also demonstrated a fundamental fact about empires: forms of inequality were not fixed.[7] This was most clear in spatial terms as regional paths fostered alternative imperial projects.[8] The cosmopolitan coast, the Muslim interior and heterodox frontiers rose to the Ottoman scene in an interactive manner, and clashed over resources, values and the nature of state at the turn of the twentieth century. With the Second Constitutional Revolution, imperial options seemed clear: a *cosmopolitan empire* with a strong record of non-Muslim rights and global connections, a *Muslim state* that marries Islam with state modernity and gives more representation to Arabs, or a *weak Ottoman political framework* that leaves local autonomy untouched.

On a different note, the coastal model questioned the historical integrity of the Middle East and provided ample evidence to the Mediterranean idea. As Faruk Tabak's life-time work vividly demonstrated, the world economy and ecological change played an instrumental role in this transformation.[9] Crop types, trade links and climate patterns were important components that forged the unity of the Mediterranean.[10] This study demonstrate that the unique identity of the (eastern) Mediterranean world consolidated only when global flows fostered cosmopolitan rule. Cosmopolitan rule was not simply the confirmation of multicultural identities. It was a historical setting that required active local agents who used global flows in their favor at the expense of political centers.[11]

The trajectory idea also sheds new light on Ottoman citizenship, imperial decline and modern state formation. It shows that the evolution of Ottoman citizenship followed a path-dependent character during the nineteenth century.[12] There is enough evidence to conclude that censuses, taxation and mass conscription achieved the least success in the frontier. Meanwhile, the Ottoman conscription drive made a breakthrough in the Turkish interior, recruiting rural peasants from the Anatolian heartland. This pattern was also consistent with the development of professional staff in the army, who overwhelmingly came from the interior towns of Anatolia and Syria. Meanwhile, the Ottoman state counted and taxed the coast better than other places, yet was forced to back down under rival pressures that stemmed from the 1838 trade treaty, communal arrangements (Mount Lebanon) or regional discontent (Macedonia).

Charles Tilly suggested some time ago that empires cease to exist because of external conquest and internal defection.[13] Fitting nicely into this schema, imperialism and nationalism have long served the fields of Ottoman and Middle Eastern Studies to justify Ottoman demise. Attrition, in the words of Alexander Motyl, was an Ottoman pattern in which imperial territories were taken away in bits and pieces over time.[14] Still, these theories of (inevitable) decline missed one crucial point: why did actual Ottoman collapse come from the most remote part of the empire? The trajectory approach demonstrates that this was the case because of severe agency problems and geopolitical competition in the far frontiers, which in turn provided a political opportunity space for its most threatened actor, the Sharif of Mecca, to go beyond the autonomy framework.[15]

Finally, nation-state failures in the Middle East during the interwar era are usually attributed to domestic political figures or ill-intentioned European designs. The trajectory model underlines another aspect. It suggests that the eclectic nature of state formation contributed to the process as well. Eclectism came into effect when several layers of the same trajectory or rival trajectories were bundled together in post-Ottoman states.[16] The subsequent spatial tensions between political centers and locals nicely illustrate that new states were less than homogeneous during the 1920s, and that powerful regional networks continued to have a different idea when it came to politics, economy and the state.[17]

A New Research Agenda

This project was written to set up an ambitious research agenda. The main goal was not to add new empirical findings or simply import a new theoretical approach into late Ottoman Studies. My idea was to offer a novel way of understanding the Middle East based on previous historical research and fresh analytical tools borrowed from social sciences and global history. In doing so, I departed from nationalist accounts, state-centered imperial narratives, center-periphery frameworks, and local history studies that have characterized the field in the last fifty years.

The new research agenda that I propose here requires a spatial, path-dependent and comparative approach. Accordingly, the next task at hand is to work around conceptual categories and make several comparisons. We need conceptually-oriented and theoretically-driven comparisons to understand imperial variation in the late Ottoman world. I believe it is only then we can have a better grasp on the meaning of empire, detect regional differences across imperial territories, and place the Ottomans into the same analytical scale as their counterparts. The historical trajectory framework offers several new venues for future research in this regard.

One such project is to develop comparisons within each trajectory. The idea would be to explore internal hierarchies and find out the degree of institutionalization in each path. A comparison between far and near frontiers can reveal the changing boundaries of central rule in the frontiers and unpack the content of local autonomy discourses. Likewise, port-city–hinterland comparison can show the strengths and weaknesses of the coastal model by examining forms of connectivity and points of contention between the two spatial units. In the interior, it would be a helpful exercise to capture the changing relationship between provincial capital cities, rising smaller market towns, and the countryside. For instance, how did Damascus fare vis-à-vis Homs and Hawran as the interior regime set in?

A second project worth pursuing is to compare Ottoman trajectories. The main goal would be to flesh out the distinctive features of each regional path by examining variation over space or key processes. An intriguing project in this regard would be to compare Izmir, Damascus and Sana'a, which represented each Ottoman path at its best. Simply put, what kind of a difference did it make to be at the center of global flows, urban Muslim rule or frontier insurgency by 1900? A comparative project on taxation, legitimacy or social mobility would serve a similar purpose and register the diverse experience of imperial subjects along trajectory lines.

Trajectory comparison can also yield insights about the possible directions that the Ottoman Empire could have taken without a war decade (1912–1922). There are three historical trends that such a counterfactuality should take into account. First, the Ottoman interior was emerging as a rival institutional setting to the globally-connected cosmopolitan coast under the reign of Abdulhamid II. Second, while the near frontier was becoming more attuned with the interior model, the far frontier was moving away from the empire. Third, the Second Constitutional Movement that relied on the coastal space and promoted middle-class ideals defined itself against interior coalitions and the frontier regimes in 1908. The challenge would be to find the fault lines between Ottoman regional paths and locate the Young Turk regime at the center of these issues.

A third comparative project can evaluate the nineteenth-century experiences of overland empires through a trajectory model. For instance, how did these empires fare in the borderlands? A comparison of tools, strategies and contexts can reveal how much imperial frontiers had in common.[18] Frontier Islam was an ideological base that has to be taken into account. On a similar ground, imperial strength can be re-evaluated based on the scope of interior regimes. I believe that the extent to which overland empires integrated resources and cultural frames into imperial settings determined their degree of survival.[19] A fruitful direction in this regard would be to examine imperial education, conscription and religious life from a comparative perspective.

I would like to finish the comparative discussion with a final note. So far, my suggestions for future projects have concentrated on "trajectories proper". Another interesting question that comes out of this framework is the fate of transition/conflict zones. These were the places where different trajectories intersected, co-existed, or had a contested relationship. Elites were divided, economic forms were multiple, and cultural identities mattered. Examining transition/conflict zones can provide fresh insights into inter communal relations in the late Ottoman Empire. When there were no path-dependent settings with clear guidelines, how did social groups manage to cooperate or perhaps clash with one another?[20] Located between the interior and frontier regimes, Sivas province in eastern Anatolia can be an excellent starting point to think about these issues.

This book has tried to convince the reader that the three-trajectory approach is worth the effort of rethinking the late Ottoman Empire and the Middle East during the nineteenth century. I believe that the book will accomplish its goal if it opens up a debate in Ottoman Studies and stimulates new empirical research. It will be up to others to improve, revise and challenge the analytical-category–historical-reality pairs offered in this study.

NOTES

Introduction

1 Pagden (2008).
2 On the idea of path-dependency, see Pierson (2000); Mahoney (2004).
3 Take the evolution of the free-trade regime into a world-historical path during the nineteenth century. Once a free-trade treaty was signed, weak states had to observe the treaty or face the gunboat diplomacy of Britain. As the century progressed, undoing the free-trade path became a more distant option as domestic actors emerged on the horizon with strong ties to the global economy. For the first point, see Horowitz (2005).
4 Turning points are only known after the fact and form the basis for 'eventful' history. See Abbott (1997); Sewell (2005) respectively.
5 Thelen (1999).
6 While military pressure (early or late) determined the patrimonial or bureaucratic content of European states, the nature of the local government (centrally-administered or participatory) held the key to whether a political regime would be absolutist or constitutional. According to Ertman (1997), Britain was bureaucratic–constitutionalist, France was patrimonia–absolutist, Germany was bureaucratic–absolutist, and Hungary was patrimonial–constitutionalist.
7 According to Mahoney (2001), there was radical liberalism in Guatemala and El Salvador, reformist liberalism in Costa Rica, and aborted liberalism in Honduras and Nicaragua.

8 Stark and Bruszt (1998).
9 On state-formation patterns in Latin America, see Centeno (2002). For the regional origins of fascism in Italy, Riley (2005). A discussion on European welfare regimes is available in Esping-Andersen (1990).
10 For a critique of these positions, see Tilly (2001); Tilly (1995).
11 My understanding of the elite reflects on the power-elite concept developed by C. W. Mills half a century ago. See Mills (1956). On power types, see Mann (1986–1993).
12 Review (1993).
13 Hourani (1968).
14 Sırma (1980). On regime stability which is tied to the perception of an effective–just ruler and unified–loyal elites, see Goldstone (2001).
15 Anscombe (1997).
16 Tabak (1988). The rise of landholding interests was a general pattern in land-abundant-and-labor-scarce economies of the Third World at the last quarter of the nineteenth century. Williamson (2002).
17 Note the distinct type of sovereignty deficit in each path. Ottomans could not establish effective control (domestic sovereignty) in the frontiers and compromised its international legal sovereignty in the Arabian Peninsula. On the coast, the key issues were the loss of control over commodity flows (interdependence sovereignty) and the erosion of Westphalian sovereignty because of extra-territoriality. For a comparison of four types of sovereignty, see Krasner (1999), pp 3–42.
18 Tilly (2005).
19 New economic sociology promotes a sociology of markets that takes networks, cultural conventions and political economy seriously. For an earlier formulation, see Granovetter (1985); see also American Behavioral Scientist (2007). The application of these ideas into economic history is in Greif (2006).
20 Levi (1997), pp 16–30.
21 Stinchcombe (1997).
22 On principal–agent problems, see Kiser (1999). For the latter point, see Brustein and Levi (1987).
23 For a state-of-the-art introduction, see McAdam, Tarrow and Tilly (2001). On the importance of pre-existing network ties to create collective action, see Gould (1995).
24 Pamuk (2006). For a defense of this position, see North (1990); Olson (1993). For other institutional explanations, see Kuran (2011); Bates (2001).

25 Wong (2001). Ingram and Clay (2000) gave theoretical support to this argument by showing that institutional patterns rely first and foremost on private norms and decentralized initiatives.
26 On frontiers, see Khodarkovsky (2002); Brower and Lazzerini (eds) (1997). For a useful introduction to maritime scholarship, see AHR Forum (2006).
27 Gieryn (2000).
28 For an organizational approach to governance and hierarchy, see Cooley (2005).
29 For a recent exception that attempts to understand the diverse character of Ottoman territories during the 1700–1850 period, see Khoury (2008).
30 On legacy literature, see the collection of essays edited by Brown and Karpat. Both volumes correct the misperceptions about the Ottoman Empire, deal with the Ottoman imprint outside Turkey, and reinterpret the transition from empire to nation state in the context of the Turkish Republic. Brown (ed) (1996); Karpat (ed) (2000).

Chapter 1 Historiography

1 For a three-wave periodization of African historiography that emphasizes political structure, economy and culture, see Cooper (2002).
2 Quataert (2005); Zürcher (2004); Ahmad (2003); Faroqhi (1999), pp 174–203.
3 For a critical reading of Middle Eastern historiography, see Lockman (2004), pp 99–272.
4 Lewis (2002); Davison (1990).
5 For thematic discussions and/or critical treatments of the meaning, application and impact of Tanzimat, see Alkan (ed) (2004); Yıldız (ed) (1992); İnalcık and Seyitdanlıoğlu (eds) (2006). On reforms, see Davison (1963).
6 On legal change and economic institutions, see Toprak (2007); Toprak (1992).
7 Shaw (1971).
8 Shaw and Shaw (1977).
9 Findley (1980); Findley (1989); Ortaylı (1983).
10 Lewis (1961). This observation was the central claim of the political-modernization school and was used for a long time to explain the

political origins of modern Turkey. For a representative account, see Kalaycıoğlu and Sarıbay (eds) (1986).
11 Ragin (1987), p 53.
12 On eulogies to the modernization project in the Turkish Republic, see Lewis (1955); Robinson (1965).
13 For the first two events, see Aktepe (1958); Ma'oz (1968), pp 29, 200–205, 226–240.
14 Berkes (1964).
15 Mardin (1973).
16 Mardin (1997).
17 There are intellectual companions from Russian and Chinese historiographies. Riasanovsky (1963); Spence (1990).
18 On the ideological premises of the modernization school, see Duara (1995), pp 17–50.
19 For recent attempts in this direction, see Özdemir (2003); Çadırcı (1991).
20 McMichael (2000), pp 79–187.
21 For a good formulation, see Keyder (1987), pp 25–48.
22 İslamoğlu-İnan (ed) (1987).
23 World-systems analysts disagree with this reading of Ottoman economic history and suggest that Ottoman–European trade started to expand earlier in the century. The two positions are available in Kurmuş (1974) and New Perspectives on Turkey (1992).
24 For an early formulation, see Parvus Efendi (1977).
25 On three forms of integration, see Pamuk (1987); Pamuk (1992); Pamuk (2006b).
26 Owen (1981).
27 Kasaba (1988).
28 Issawi (1999). On the ethnic division of labor idea, Sussnitzki (1966). Note that this reading of economic entrepreneurship was based on a supply-side approach that credited cultural traits. For a fuller understanding, see Thornton (1999).
29 On the first point, see Keyder and Tabak (eds) (1991). For regional case studies, Owen (ed) (2000). On political outcomes, Gerber (1987). See also Macauley (2009) for a positive evaluation of Ottoman Land Code from a comparative perspective.
30 This thesis has been fully developed and documented for Anatolia by Donald Quataert in the 1990s, see Quataert (1993).

31 For a demonstration from Ottoman Bulgaria, see Palairet (1997), pp 58–84.
32 The resistance of peasants in the countryside, worker struggles in the cities, and the political alliances between Young Turks and urban guilds are discussed in Quataert (1983). For a collection of essays on Ottoman working class and labor history, see Quataert and Zürcher (eds) (1995).
33 For a theoretical statement about the earlier origins of Ottoman incorporation, see Kasaba and Wallerstein (1980).
34 Ahmad (1980); Toprak (1982).
35 Keyder (1988); Keyder (1994).
36 For economic performance arguments that put Asia on an equal footing with Europe, see Pomeranz (2000). For the mismatch between Western categories and non-Western experience, see Wong (2006). Against east–west binaries, see Islamoğlu and Perdue (2009). For a critique of this literature, Bryant (2006).
37 For a superb study, see Kayalı (1997).
38 The "overdue survival" of the Ottoman Empire is usually attributed to Great Power rivalry in the age of imperialism that manifested itself in the Eastern Question. The classic account is in Anderson (1966).
39 For a demonstration, see Khoury (1983); Reilly (2002); Köksal (2002).
40 The resilience of local economic actors is described in various contexts. On Transjordan, Rogan (1999). On Iraq, Shields (2000); Fattah (1997). On Yemen, Blumi (2003b).
41 Doumani (1995).
42 Deringil (1998).
43 Rogan (2004); Fortna (2002); Roded (1986).
44 This dimension of late Ottoman rule and its demise during the Turkish Republic has been captured in recent articles, see Kasaba (2006); Birtek (2007).
45 Salzmann (2004). The more general and theoretical argument is in Salzmann (1993).
46 Barkey (2005).
47 For a defense of this position, see Abou-El-Haj (2005), pp 44–46, 54, 57–60, 78, 86–92.
48 Makdisi (2000), pp 52, 1–14, 146–165; Makdisi (2002a). See also, Deringil (2003).

49 Hanioğlu (2008a); Hanioğlu (2008b).
50 On Young Turk ideology, see Worringer (2004).
51 Barkey (2008), p 1.
52 For a comprehensive account, see Faroqhi (ed) (2006).
53 The power of nationalism on the historiography of the Ottoman Empire should not be underestimated. Two diametrically opposed myths still underline Pax Ottomanica and the Ottoman dark ages. The former speaks of justice and peace, the latter perceives the same reality as foreign occupation and constant decay. On the Balkans, see Adanır (2000). On Arab lands, see Abou-El-Haj (1982); Reilly (1999).
54 Thomas Metcalf formulated this position very cogently in the context of British Empire: "once the historian sets foot on the colonial shore, however, the focus of attention abruptly narrows. In most accounts of colonialisms, each colony is assumed to exist only in its relationship to the imperial center. These studies in effect conceive of the British Empire as a set of strings – or better yet, as lines of telegraph wire through which information flows up and policy directives flow down- running from each colony to the metropole in London. The history of each colony is thus written in isolation from those of its neighbors." Metcalf (2007), p 6.

Chapter 2   Coast

1 Faroqhi (1991); Stoianovich (1953).
2 Frangakis-Syrett (1992), pp 156, 216–217.
3 For this point, see Keyder (1991). On Acre, Philipp (2002).
4 Frangakis-Syrett (1999), p 23.
5 On the role of embeddedness in economic action, Granovetter (1985). For the social origins of economic processes, see Nee and Swedberg (eds) (2005).
6 On silk-reeling factories of Lebanon, see Owen (1987). On Greek and Jewish capital, see respectively, Exertzoglou (1999); Gounaris (1993).
7 Fawaz (1983), pp 65–66; Issawi (1977). On Bursa and western Anatolia, see Quataert (1987); Kurmuş (1987).
8 Stoianovich (1960).
9 Clay (1994).
10 Monopolies were the norm in long-distance trade in early modern Europe. By the late nineteenth century, oligopolies became dominant

especially in capital-intensive industries. Meanwhile, the joint stock company emerged as the new business unit to pool large amounts of capital.

11 Quataert (1995).
12 Note its positive impact on real daily wages which increased more than 45 percent between 1880 and 1910s – at least – in the imperial capital. Özmucur and Pamuk (2002).
13 On port-town development, see Seikaly (2002); Yenişehirlioğlu (2002); Yolalıcı (1998) for Haifa, Mersin and Samsun respectively. Contrast this pattern with the earlier development of Trabzon on the Black Sea coast, which benefited from extraordinary political conditions (Crimean War) and relied on regional transit trade with Tabriz. For the rise and fall of Trabzon, see Turgay (1993).
14 On coastal rivalries, see Haddad (1998). On social crisis in Haifa and Jaffa at the turn of the century, see Agmon (2003).
15 For a detailed account on Mersin's exports items, see Toksöz (2004). On Palestine, Buheiry (1981); Schölch (1981).
16 In addition to coastal markets, the other pull factor was increasing demand from Europe. For the big picture, see O'Rouke (1997).
17 Toledano (1997). The Maronite Church and the Shihab Emirs played a similar role in Lebanon. Leeuwen (1991). For a recent study on Shiite tax-farmers of Lebanon that unveils the historical origins of Druze–Maronite rivalry, see Winter (2010). On the long-term impact of imperial administrative restructing in Lebanon, see Hanssen (2005) and Akarlı (1993), which underline economic benefits and positive political outcomes respectively.
18 Fawaz (1998).
19 Horowitz (2005).
20 Zachs (2004).
21 On local debates/perceptions about Westernization, see Exertzoglou (2003); Exertzoglou (2007); Mardin (1974).
22 Abu-Maneh (1980); Zachs (2005), pp 50–85.
23 Mardin (1962); Hourani (1962).
24 Khuri-Makdisi (2003), p 214.
25 On scapegoating, see Emrence (1999); Turgut (2002). On juvenile delinquency, Mazower (2005), pp 230–231.
26 For a comparison, see Mitchell (1988).
27 The controversy over Alliance Israelite Universelle schools within the Jewish community of Salonica clearly demonstrates what was at stake for the middle classes. For a rich discussion, see Molho (1992).

28 Hanssen (2004). Not all the municipality experiments of local actors were successful. For a failure of this sort in Istanbul, see Rosenthal (1980). Still, compare the better Ottoman record with that of Tunis. See Cleveland (1978).
29 On Beirut and Alexandria, see Khuri-Makdisi (2003), pp 96–176. For a similar reading, Ostle (2002).
30 For an extensive discussion, see Kramer (2008). Not all Europeans were merchants. Fuhrmann (2003). On seasonal labor migration, Kasaba (1991); Clay (1998).
31 Europeans contributed to social diversity especially in Izmir and Alexandria. Beirut and Salonica hosted only 5–6,000 Europeans at this time. It is interesting to note that the demographic weight of Europeans was correlated negatively with domestic-reform calls in the Ottoman port-city. On cultural diversity in the port-city, see Zandi-Sayek (2001).
32 Firro (1990).
33 The influential Evrenos family tried to weather the storm by attaching itself to provincial bureaucracy in Salonica province. On the Evrenos family, Özdemir (2003).
34 For the latter point, see Makdisi (2000), pp 67–95.
35 On the middle-peasantry thesis, see Pamuk (2008), pp 3–95. Contrast this pattern with the Egyptian hinterland, which experienced waves of peasant resistance because of its integration to the world economy via large agricultural units specialized in cotton. While large landholdings "freed" the peasantry from means of production, mono-crop culture made them dependent on the vagaries of the market.
36 Note the increasing brigandage activity in the hinterland with wealth accumulation on the coast. As Halil Dural showed for western Anatolia, bands were fictive kinship organizations that provided localized racketeering services in return for prestige and material rewards. In doing so, they functioned as a petty form of wealth-sharing mechanism especially for refugees and recently sedentarized populations. There was no communal message involved. This pattern is consistent with the nature of brigandage activity in the Balkans during the nineteenth century where brigands always switched sides between the Ottomans and the newly-founded Greek state. Koliopoulos (1987). On western Anatolia, see Dural (1999).
37 On the Muslim bourgeoisie thesis, see Karpat (2001), pp 89–116.

38 The hinterland of Salonica was at the center of competition between rival nationalist organizations and subsequently fell prey to Ottoman oppression, Bulgarian terrorism, Greek irredentism and Serbian cultural activity. The difference-maker was the political agency that brokered a collective action agenda out of communal tensions. Most importantly, the Internal Macedonian Revolutionary Organization skillfully exploited the unsolved agrarian question. Deep disagreements in European circles about the future of Macedonia and the inability of the Ottoman state to control private means of violence further heartened the rebel sides to continue fighting. See Adanır (2001).
39 Yazbak (1998), pp 112–162; Yazbak (1998).
40 In most situations, the Land Question was the key to communal tensions. On Jewish–Arab conflict in Jaffa, see LeVine (2004). On Greek–Turkish tensions in Ayvalık, see Terzibaşıoğlu (2001). On the rise of local Greek interests in Samsun, see Issawi (1999).
41 This is partly why, unlike the major port-cities in the empire, regional port-towns failed to project their influence over the hinterlands. The power of landed interests in Çukurova plain is a case in point.
42 On the socialist politics of Salonica, see Dumont (1999). On working-class power in Salonica, Izmir, Jaffa and Haifa during the interwar period, see Mazower (1991), pp 115–128; Emrence (2006), pp 66–69, 100, 115; Lockman (1997).
43 On the Jewish porters of Salonica, see Quataert (2002).
44 For the theoretical point, see Katznelson (1985). On the extra-economic origins of union durability, see the comparative work of Kimeldorf (1988).
45 Quataert (1994b).
46 Chalcraft (2002; 2004) recently showed that the cab drivers of Cairo who had neither guild backgrounds nor class organizations used strikes to survive in the city.
47 Keyder (1988). The Greek bourgeoisie was not terribly interested in state reform. Kasaba (1994); Kasaba (1993).
48 Despite a better performance towards the end of the century, the Ottomans remained poor tax-collectors. The ratio of tax revenues to total GDP stayed around 11 percent before World War I, with approximately one third of state income coming from trade between 1887 and 1907. Shaw (1975). Compare this trend with Latin America

where the state was also weak but relied on trade-based taxes. See Centeno (1997).
49 Ottoman cosmopolitanism went hand-in-hand with the installation of new hierarchies in the port-city. The modernization of the landscape and urban-renewal efforts contributed to the physical extension of the Ottoman city, yet led to the polarization of the urban space. Social class and communal identity were at the center of this transformation. In a few decades, the repackaging of the city reinforced the ethno–religious divide in Izmir and Istanbul, consolidated class divisions within each *millet* in Salonica, and paved the way for the establishment of working-class neighborhoods and immigrant settlements in and around major Ottoman cities. On the economic logic of urban planning in Istanbul, see Çelik (1986).
50 Keyder (1999).

Chapter 3 Interior

1 For the classic formulation, see Hourani (1968), esp. pp 45, 48–49. The Muslim bloc drew its strength from former military families, religious functionaries (*ulema*) and local merchants. The first group included lesser ayans, former janissary leaders (aghas) and local governors. Dominating the *ilmiye* posts, the religious *ulema* consisted of the judiciary and the descendants of the prophet family. As late-comers, merchants would rise to prominence and join the Muslim bloc towards the end of the nineteenth century.
2 For Ottoman settlement policy in northern and central Syria, see Lewis (1987), pp 3–37, 58–73. On Syrian province, Abu-Manneh (1992).
3 Yazbak (1997).
4 Schölch (1984).
5 Gould (1976). Still, the Armenians built a successful resistance to Ottoman rule in the same mountainous region. For a detailed discussion of the Zeytun revolts, see Günay (2007), pp 223–347.
6 Schilcher (1991).
7 Khoury (1991).
8 Masters (1988); Masters (1992).
9 On missionary activity, see Makdisi (2008); Makdisi (2004); Farah (1986). On land ownership, see Rafeq (2000).

10 Khoury (1983), esp. pp 43–44.
11 Reilly (1989).
12 Thompson (1993).
13 The Bicker faction had seven family members sitting in the Amsterdam government. On Dutch patrimonialism, see Adams (2005), p 99.
14 On Aleppo, see Watenpaugh (2006), 38–39. On Jerusalem, see Pappé (1997).
15 On Ankara, Safad and Hama, see respectively, Köksal (2002); Abbasi (2005); Reilly (2002).
16 Doumani (2003); Doumani (1998).
17 Consolidating power through networks, it is no coincidence that the Medici of Florence also built strong ties around kinship, marriage and economic relations, while relegating political patronage to weak ties. Padgett and Ansell (1993).
18 Fortna (2002).
19 Roded (1986).
20 On forms of cultural diffusion regarding architectural styles, naming practices and language choices, see Weber (2002); Hudson (2008), pp 33–44.
21 There has been growing research on several aspects of tax-farming practices in the Ottoman Empire. For a comprehensive account, see Genç (2000). For fiscal, economic and political perspectives, see respectively, Pamuk (2007), pp 133–139; Rafeq (1984); Salzmann (2004).
22 The networked character of the Ottoman tax-farming world stemmed from the temporary, political and immobile nature of the Ottoman tax-farm. No single investor was in a position to acquire and operate the tax-farm on an individual basis. This would have required economic resources, political connections, and direct supervision at the same time.
23 On the late Ottoman property regime from a comparative perspective, see İslamoğlu (ed) (2004).
24 On northern Iraq and Baghdad, see respectively, Shields (1992); Shields (1991); Fattah (1991).
25 Weber (2004).
26 On Muslim merchant power, Gilbar (2003).
27 Doumani (1995), esp. pp 29, 55–65, 214.

28 On regional markets and local merchants, see Reilly (1992); Tabak (1988).
29 Faroqhi (1991b).
30 The making of Anatolian economic integration is explored in Quataert (1977).
31 Faroqhi (1991b).
32 On economic and political nationalism of grain merchants, see Ökçün (1997); Provence (2005), esp. p 133.
33 Masters (1999).
34 On Aleppo, see Sluglett (2002). On Damascus, Reilly (1993). On Anatolia, Quataert (1994a).
35 Quataert (1988).
36 Faroqhi (2009), pp 186–188.
37 On manufacturing, see Quataert (1997); Quataert (1993). For the economic performance of the Ottoman Balkans, Palairet (1997).
38 On a similar note, the relationship between *vakıf*, the real-estate market, and the Muslim bloc is still waiting to be explored. This will be crucial to understanding urban economic hierarchies at the second half of the nineteenth century.
39 Schilcher (1985).
40 For an account of this sort, see Lapidus (1989).
41 Masters (1990); Rafeq (1988).
42 Protestors left the Jewish neighborhoods and poor Christians untouched during the turmoil. See Harel (1998).
43 Masters (2001), pp 130–168.
44 For the example of al-Nimrs in Nablus, see Gilbar (1998).
45 As the major beneficiaries of Ottoman political institutions and the land regime, core members of the Muslim bloc sought imperial patronage, while carefully maintaining their position as an intermediary group. Guided by ideas of social engineering, the military wing of the Arab-imperial class demanded change and was more interested in penetrating society. Merchants of smaller scale and religious figures on the periphery of Ottoman religious establishment were less keen on state penetration and felt closer to localist visions and religious renewal programs.
46 Vatter (2006).
47 Vatter (1994).
48 Gould (1995) underlines the importance of informal social ties and spatial proximity on collective action. See Gould (1995), esp. pp 114, 118, 205–206.

49 Williamson (2002) shows that commodity–price convergence in the late nineteenth century turned wage-rental ratios against workers in land-abundant-and-labor-scarce economies. In the Ottoman case, this was at least partially true until 1890, as the 30-year moving averages of real wages show a decline between 1850 and 1890. Özmucur and Pamuk (2002).
50 Aminzade and McAdam (2001).
51 Wong (1997), p 44.
52 Grehan (2003).
53 Ma'oz (1968), p 185. For the eighteenth century, see Grehan (2007), pp 75–78.
54 Quataert (1991).
55 Greene (2005).
56 For instance, Ottomans had a shaky relationship with the local elite in Jerusalem. On Ottoman reservations about local notables in Jerusalem, see Kusher (1996).

Chapter 4 Frontier

1 There is growing interest to understand Ottoman borderlands. See the special issue of the International Journal of Turkish Studies (2003) for the early modern period, and the MIT Electronic Journal of Middle East Studies (2003) for the experience of Arab provinces during the nineteenth century.
2 Çetinsaya (2003); Deringil (1990).
3 Reinkowski (2003).
4 For this argument, see Makdisi (2002a); Deringil (2003).
5 He was appalled by local beliefs in Tikrit, criticized "oriental ways" of doing business in Mosul, and described in detail lack of urban planning in Baghdad. Ali Bey (2003), pp 58, 66–67, 76–85. For the perceptions of Ottoman statesmen and intellectuals towards the frontiers, see Herzog (2002); Kühn (2002).
6 The Hijaz Railway was an Ottoman enterprise in terms of its funding and workforce, and its construction shared a similar geopolitical rationale with that of the Trans-Siberian Railway. Ochsenwald (1980); Gülsoy (1994).
7 The late Ottoman Empire suffered from high transportation costs. Imperial roads were in rudimentary condition, shipping was under the

control of the Europeans, and the railroads did not last long enough to deliver long-term benefits to the empire. For an account that treats the evolution of Ottoman transport systems against the backdrop of European imperialism, the world economy, and the modernizing Ottoman state, see Mentzel (2006).

8. The Mexican state used similar strategies against Maya in the Yucatan Peninsula. In both the Druze and Mayan cases, the central state built roads, sent expeditionary forces, stationed military troops, and created new administrative units to quell community-based resistance in the frontiers at the turn of the twentieth century. On the Maya, see Curtin (2000), pp 86–88.

9. Farouk-Sluglett and Sluglett (1991); Farouk-Sluglett and Sluglett (1983), pp 491–505.

10. An observer of Ottoman Iraq, Longrigg had a similar list of recommendations: "settle your tribes on the land; help them to irrigate by canals; give them security of hold; tax lightly and justly and allow no trespass against those you have settled ..." Longrigg (1925/1968), p 289.

11. Mandaville (1986).

12. Koloğlu (2003), p xxvii. On tribal school experience, see Rogan (1996).

13. For a demonstration from Iraq, see Çetinsaya (2006), pp 49–71.

14. Herzog (2003).

15. For a different reading of pan-Islamism, see Aydın (2007).

16. Trust did not solve the problems of the central Ottoman authority. On the contrary, as high trusters with no full access to local information, the Ottomans became big risk takers and paid the price dearly with the revolt of Mecca Sharif in 1916. It is telling that Turkish memory later constructed the Sharif as an untrustworthy character! For a relational account on trust, see Cook, Hardin and Levi (2005).

17. Bruinessen (1992), pp 192–195; Çetinsaya (2005).

18. On Kurdish emirates, see Jwaideh (2006), pp 54–74; on intra-emirate conflicts, see Hakan (2007); on religious entrepreneurs, see Olson (1989), p 3.

19. For a political history of the Druze, see Firro (1992), pp 206–244. On the rise of al-Atrash clan, see Firro (2005).

20. Created after Ottoman collapse, Transjordan is in fact a historical misnomer. Transjordan was a transition zone between southern Syria

NOTES

and Hijaz province at the turn of the twentieth century. For a comparative analysis of Transjordan that shows imperial instruments of rule and regional forms of integration in the north and their absence in southern districts, see Rogan (1998).

21 On Ottoman responses, Anscombe (1997); Kurşun (1998), pp 133–193.
22 The global trend should also be kept in mind. Local resistance movements intensified across the globe when the weapons gap between imperial centers and local subjects declined rapidly, imperial ideologies became less inclusive, and geopolitical competition provided a political opportunity space for insurgents in the age of imperialism.
23 The main goal of the supergovernor–inspector was to pacify insurgency. A detailed discussion on the political responsibilities of Ahmet Şakir Paşa is available in, Karaca (1993).
24 For an innovative reading of Midhat Paşa's political carreer, see Abu-Manneh (1998).
25 Çetinsaya (2006), p 17. A similar situation existed in Yemen, Farah (2002), p 112.
26 Pamuk (2006a).
27 On the predatory nature of protection rackets, see Tilly (1985). For the relationship between monopolization of violence and economic growth, see Temin (2005). For brokerage functions, see Blok (1974).
28 Shahvar (2003).
29 Nalbandian (1963), pp 78–79.
30 Marufoğlu (1998), p 156.
31 Great Britain, Foreign Office (1920), p 29.
32 Leaderships of heterodox religious communities faced several challenges in the region. These confrontations included Druze peasants against the Al-Atrash clan (1889–1890), Ismaili peasants against Ismaili amirs (1916–1917), and Yazidi Kurds against Mirs (1930s).
33 Blumi (2003a).
34 Dasnabedian (1990), p 66.
35 Baldry (1976b).
36 Jwaideh (1984).
37 Haj (1997), p 26.
38 Batatu (1978).
39 Fuccaro (1999).
40 Shields (1991).

41 Rogan (1999), pp 95–121.
42 There were urban, mercantile and/or coastal interests in places such as Jidda, Hudayda, Baghdad, Basra and Diyarbakır. Yet, for institutional, geographical and demographic reasons, they were not able to shape the frontier trajectory. For eighteenth century Basra with its vibrant trade connections, see Abdullah (2000).
43 It is no coincidence that two robust findings about civil wars (1945–1999) were the presence of rough terrain and the superior local knowledge of insurgents. Fearon and Laitin (2003).
44 Ochsenwald (1984), p 34.
45 Foggo (2002).
46 Khoury and Kostiner (eds) (1990).
47 For the distinction between interactive and symbolic networks, see Watts (2004).
48 Gellner (1981), pp 44, 56.
49 This stands in sharp contrast to the political articulation of religion in the interior path, where an *ulema*-controlled urban Islam reproduced the existing social order. For a similar argument, see Ocak (2003).
50 Take the example of the Mahdist movement and its transformation into a state in late nineteenth-century Sudan. The movement was driven by demands for religious purity and found key supporters among nomads and slave traders, who opposed the modernizing and expanding Egyptian state. Mahdist military victories, promises of low taxation, and the chances of booty convinced more tribes to join the rebel camp along clan lines. While Mahdi introduced a Sharia court to dispense justice, the revolutionary experience turned into a struggle between rival clan factions first, then evolved into a personalist rule backed up by ruler's kinsmen (who he later replaced by Mamluk-type imperial guards). While Mahdiship as a movement shared many characteristics with far-frontier politics in late Ottoman times, the nature of the Mahdi state presented striking similarities with the political history of the Arabian Peninsula in the interwar era. On the Mahdist state, see Holt and Daly (2000).
51 Bang (1996), pp 143–188. A detailed comparison with the Sanusiyya of Libya can lead to interesting conclusions.
52 Baldry (1976a).
53 For the mobilizing impact of fear and threat on contentious politics, see Goldstone and Tilly (2001). As Gould (1996) has shown in the context of the Whiskey Rebellion (1774), elites were likely to rebel

when they had no ties to federal patronage or had a clientele that overlapped with those of the federal officials.
54 For high discount rates and transaction costs that turn rebellions into easy choices, see Levi (1988), pp 1–40; on "pre-conditions" of a successful rebellion, see Brustein and Levi (1987).
55 Jwaideh (1963).
56 Resistance movements in eastern Anatolia and northern Iraq were organized by *Nakşibendi* sufi şeyhs. Still, note the pro-state record of *Nakşibendi-Khalidi* orders. They fought against Salafi–Wahhabi expansion, Christian uprisings, and other "heretical" movements since the 1820s. On the latter point, see Abu-Manneh (2003); Weismann (2001), pp 52–54.
57 According to some estimates, the tribal regiments were organized in 65 units and had 50,000 members. On Hamidiye regiments, see Klein (2002).
58 The six Ottoman provinces (Vilayet-i Sitte) were Bitlis, Elazığ, Van, Erzurum, Sivas, and Diyarbakır.
59 For two different positions on the topic that reach to the same conclusion. See Salt (1993); Mann (2005), pp 111–179.
60 On the perspective of the Bedirhan family, see Bozarslan (ed) (1991).
61 Bedirhan of Botan played an instrumental role in terminating other Kurdish emirates in the region. He eliminated his regional rivals (Nurullah Bey of Hakkari and Şeref Bey of Bitlis) and waged a military campaign against Nestorians. It was only after Bedirhan's territorial expansion that the Ottoman state was in a position to end the rule of Kurdish emirates in the region.
62 Gould (1976).
63 Kılıç (2006).
64 While gatekeepers controlled access to community resources, itinerant brokers were outsiders who united the frontier elites around a common resistance agenda. For an insightful discussion, see Gould and Fernandez (1989).

Chapter 5 Routes of Transformation

1 Findley (1989), p 23. On changing recruitment, training and compensation patterns, see also Findley (1980).
2 Shaw (1971), pp 71–208.

3 The idea of an efficient provincial administration gained wide currency in the Ottoman Empire under competitive state pressures during the 1860s. On the domestic side, the Ottoman concern was to avoid another foreign intervention on the pretext of public disorder. Abu-Manneh (1992).
4 For a balanced account, see Fortna (2008). On cultural politics of Abdulhamid II, see Deringil (1998).
5 Hanioğlu (2008a).
6 For an insightful reading, see Tekeli and İlkin (1980). On the contribution of *dönme* families to 1908 Revolution, see Baer (2010), pp 84–101, esp. 96.
7 Worringer (2004).
8 As a counter-trend, note the significant Jewish contribution to the 1908 project. On elite input, see Ahmad (2002). On the relative weakness of Zionism in Palestine, see Campos (2005).
9 Kansu (1997), pp 193–241. The CUP drew its votes primarily from Salonica, Thrace and western Anatolia. Frontier leaderships and the urban Muslim bloc prevailed in borderlands and inland regions respectively. In contested zones like eastern Anatolia and Macedonia, Armenian revolutionaries in Van and Albanian nationalists in Kosovo also secured political support for their candidates.
10 Kayalı (1995).
11 The organizational weaknesses of Liberal Entente, its intellectual leadership, and vague political program are discussed in Birinci (1990).
12 For an overview, see Beinin (2001), pp 77–80.
13 The historiography underlines the political character of the Beirut Reform Committee, seeing it as the harbinger of Lebanese or Arab aspirations. Still, note that a large chunk of demands for provincial autonomy dealt with issues of administrative efficiency: to make financial instruments available to Beiruti mercants (loans, concessions and shareholding companies) and to upgrade the human resources of the province in line with the later findings of the Bahjat-Tamimi report.
14 For the political significance of economic boycotts in the making of Turkish nationalism, see Ahmad (1988).
15 Hailing from Shuf, the Druze Amir came from the influential Arslan family. He worked closely with CUP leadership, distrusted European

intentions for the Arab provinces, and later became an important spokesperson for the Arab/Syrian cause in Europe during the interwar period. On his autobiographical work, see Emir Şekib Arslan (2008).
16 On Muslim refugees and the Great Fire of Salonica, see respectively, McCarthy (1995), pp 156–164; Mazower (2005), pp 298–310.
17 Industry statistics were collected from Marmara and western Anatolia regions, see Ökçün (1971).
18 The founding of *Esnaf Cemiyetleri* represented an important effort on the CUP side to recruit political allies in the capital. If the mass politics of 1908 made social coalitions a practical necessity, the boycott experience showed the Committee that, if rightly manipulated and properly transformed, guilds could be of great political value. Kara Kemal demonstrated that this view was indeed correct. National companies set up by CUP worked closely with *Esnaf Cemiyetleri*.
19 On national companies, see Ahmad (1980).
20 These locations were Uşak, Afyon, Denizli, Muğla and Balıkesir. They served as key spots to mobilize the Turkish resistance against Greek advance by organizing local congresses, setting up military fronts, and operating as political units with governmental powers. In this respect, western Anatolian resistance was locally-grown and kept its autonomy from nationalist movement in Sivas. For a superb study, see Tekeli and İlkin (1989). For a revionist reading of Turkish nationalist movement, see Kayalı (2008).
21 For this point, see Firro (2003), pp 84–91. The economic concern for Muslim leaderships was the severing of commercial ties between the coast and the hinterland/interior. While the coastal Muslims of former Beirut province lost their connections with the interior towns of Syria, hinterland interests in western Anatolia feared that the Greek control of Izmir would put them into a disadvantaged position.
22 1.2 million Orthodox Christians and 0.5 million Muslims were swapped between Greece and Turkey. On various aspects of the Greco–Turkish population exchange, see Hirschon (ed) (2003); Yıldırım (2006).
23 The nationalist-middle class strategy in the eastern Mediterranean was two-fold during the 1920s: (1) nurture political amnesia to bury the cosmopolitan past, yet (2) promote economic integration to revive the coastal miracle. Christian members of the cosmopolitan Beiruti

elite also subscribed to this vision. They wanted to reaffirm the economic ties of Lebanon to world markets, yet detach it from the rest of the Arab Middle East. They imagined Lebanon as a mercantile republic, a descendant of the Phoenician empire. On the imagined past of Phoenicia, see Salibi (1988), pp 167–181.
24 On the political career and ideas of Asali, see Seikaly (1991).
25 The only exception was the use of Turkish in courts. Kayalı (1997), pp 90–91.
26 Despite several revionist accounts, the idea that CUP forcefully "Turkified" the Arab provinces is still a widely accepted view in the literature. For an early formulation, see Antonius (1938), pp 105–107.
27 This thesis is fully developed by Ernest Dawn. See Dawn (1973).
28 Take the case of Kurd Ali. As the most influential Arabist journalist in Damascus, he served the Ottoman war effort in several capacities. As he wrote in his memoirs, Kurd Ali once told a foreign diplomat that we (Arabs) would rather be with Ottomans than with any foreign power. Muhammed Kürd Ali (2006), p 119.
29 Erickson (2001); Pamuk (2005).
30 The Ottoman solution to famine and hunger was to set up a provisioning committee. The committee divided the Ottoman provinces into five economic zones, which reflected the priorities of the central state. While Istanbul alone occupied zone 1, the provinces of Adana, Aleppo, Syria, *sancak* of Jerusalem, and Lebanon fell under zone 4. Accordingly, the Arab interior received less attention from the government, and had to live with the immediate consequences of war on its own.
31 Khalidi views the war as the deathblow to Ottomanism. Khalidi (1997), pp 177–180. For autobiographical support to this argument, see Jacobson (2008).
32 On the social origins of Arabists, see Khalidi (1991). For a helpful discussion on the Iraqi aspect, see Simon (1991).
33 An ambitious project waiting the intellectual historian of the Middle East and the Ottoman Empire is to think about the new imperial class as a whole before unpacking it into nationalist elites. A good starting point might be to map out the commonalities and internal differences of this group. Among other things, this strategy can be helpful to trace the evolution of several ideological currents in the region during the interwar period.
34 Gelvin (1998), pp 87–137.

35 Watenpaugh (2006), pp 160–184.
36 The Committee's position on eastern Anatolia was highly ambiguous, reflecting a major clash between revolutionary political idealism in theory and Hobbesian realism in practice. While the former position required radical social change to uproot existing hierarchies, the latter emphasized the threat of foreign agression to keep the status quo. As such, the Committee government shared the negative Armenian view about eastern Anatolia, yet was careful enough not to alienate Kurdish and religious allies of the state in a volatile borderland region. This approach was in line with the dualism inherent in the late Ottoman frontier vision and would later become a political legacy for the Turkish Republic.
37 On the ecology of Karak revolt, see Rogan (1994).
38 The definitive study on the topic is Kayalı (1997), pp 144–173. For the political motivations behind the Sharifian Revolt, see also Wilson (1987), pp 20–25.
39 The direction and amount of British subsidies made a powerful impact on the evolution of the Sharifian Revolt and shaped several post-war outcomes in the region. The Sharif of Mecca was the major recepient of British funds during the war years, which totaled 4.3 million pounds in February 1920. The Sharif used this money to lure tribes to his political cause and find allies in the desert. In the critical post-war years, the British channeled these funds primarily to Saudi leadership. Without financial backing, Husayn became increasingly isolated in the Peninsula; his son Abdullah had to give in to several British demands in Transjordan; and Faysal found himself powerless in the wake of French advance to Damascus in 1920.
40 For competing views on the fate of Armenians, see Levy (2005); Bloxham (2005); Sonyel (2000).
41 The famous example was the Cemilpaşazades. Hailing from Diyarbakır, Ahmet Cemil Paşa (1837–1902) was the founder of the influential Cemilpaşazade family. Before returning to his hometown, he spent his life in imperial service as tax-collector, inspector and district governor in eastern Anatolia, Istanbul and Yemen. The next generation of the family received imperial education, took up bureaucratic posts, and fought on the Ottoman side during World War I. After the war, remaining family members became active in Kurdish associations such as *Kürt Teali Cemiyeti* in Diyarbakır. On the

political activities and bureaucratic service of Cemilpaşazade family, see Malmisanij (2004).
42 Özoğlu (2004), pp 87–120.
43 The Kurdish opposition came from three directions during the 1920s. All tried to incite a large-scale rebellion in eastern Anatolia, yet were ineffective on the ground or were crushed by the Turkish state. The political efforts of Kurdish officers in the Turkish army (Azadi Group) and the crossborder attack plan of the Bedirhan family (Hoybun) equally failed. With its Islamic credentials and mass following, it was harder to put down the Şeyh Said rebellion. The movement nonetheless collapsed after two months when they failed to capture Diyarbakır. On Hoybun, see Fuccaro (2003). On the Şeyh Said rebellion, see Olson (1989), pp 91–152.
44 For the economic bases of Britain's rural allies, Haj (1997), pp 27–31. On clan-based opposition to al-Atrash leadership, see Schaebler (1998).
45 Tribal lifestyle, religious purity, and frontier politics turned into contentious issues between the Saudi state and *Ikhwan* leadership, representing a clash between two modes of state formation: Ottoman frontier style on one side, and its more centralized and consolidated form on the other. On the latter point, see Kostiner (1993), pp 106–140.

Conclusion

1 On collective-action comparisons in and around the Middle East, see Barkey (1991); Burke (1991).
2 On the transitional character of the interwar era, see the seminal study by Khoury (1987).
3 Suffice it to say here that any discussion on frontiers should not be based on the "Turner thesis" or its negation, since both generalize from the North American example. For a comparative perspective and a thorough analysis, see respectively, Curtin (1999), pp 41–92; Baud and Schendel (1997).
4 South-east Asian frontiers, Manchuria and the southern Caucasus turned into troubled spots with imperial competition around 1900. Compare and contrast this trend with an earlier wave of successful imperial expansion during the eighteenth century, when Russian and

Chinese advances in the Caucasus and central Asia were not deterred by European presence, weak regional rivals (Ottoman and Iranian Empires), and competing local factions.
5 Punjabi Sikhs played a similar and perhaps a more prominent role for the British Empire. Metcalf (2007), pp 68–135.
6 Frederick Cooper brilliantly observed the general pattern. New demands were directed to the center when imperial capital becomes the agent of change. The goal is redraw the lines of inclusion and exclusion within the empire. Peripheral elites were drawn to non-imperial solutions only when this strategy did not work. For the former point, Cooper (2006), esp. p 69.
7 Stoler and McGranahan (2007), p 12.
8 For changing metropole–colony relations between the Iberian Peninsula and Latin America through slavery, see Adelman (2006), pp 56–100.
9 Tabak (2008).
10 Horden and Purcell (2006).
11 This partly explains why there were no cosmopolitan spaces during the eighteenth and twentieth centuries. Absolutist regimes, strong local leaderships, centralized rule, closed and national economies, as well as restrictions on human mobility, were detrimental to cosmopolitan rule in modern times.
12 On Ottoman citizenship, see Salzmann (1999). On censuses, Shaw (1978). On conscription, see Zürcher (1999). On taxation, see Shaw (1975).
13 Tilly (1997).
14 Motyl (2001), pp 5, 77, 87.
15 On theories of imperial overexpansion, see Snyder (1991) that discusses international pressures (realist explanation), choices of policy-makers (cognitive explanation), and the interests of domestic groups (domestic explanation) as the bases of expansion. Although more sophisticated than all three, his theory of coalition politics seems less applicable to the Ottoman case.
16 Modern Turkey incorporated the coastal, inland and frontier zones of Anatolia. The new Iraqi state consisted of near and intermediate frontiers of the defunct Ottoman Empire. Mandate Syria had to unite two types of interiors while dealing with frontier regions like Druze Mountain. Transjordan and Saudi Arabia acquired places from both

extremes of intermediate (Salt vs. Karak) and far frontier zones (Hijaz vs. Riyad) respectively.

17 Trajectory-specific tensions developed via demands for local autonomy and political representation. The former was the case in eastern Anatolia, northern Iraq, Hawran and Karak where local leaderships demanded to keep their imperial privileges and sustain the trajectory-specific character of their region. The latter was voiced in Izmir, Aleppo and Hijaz. Using conventional politics, regional leaders tried to "localize" decision-making processes vis-à-vis Ankara, Damascus and Riyad.

18 Successors of contiguous empires have faced protest and collective mobilization in the old frontiers with globalization. Kurds in eastern Anatolia, Chechnians in the Caucasus, and Tibetans in Tibet and Uigurs in Eastern Turkistan recently challenged the Turkish, Russian and Chinese states respectively.

19 For a similar argument, see the comparative work of Lieberman who suggests the presence of "synchronized trajectories" in mainland south-east Asia, Japan and Europe based on internal cohesion, state centralization and economic flows. See Lieberman (2003–2009), esp. pp 79–80 in the first volume for the theoretical point.

20 This might lead to what Charles Tilly calls mutual predation when adjacent networks compete for the same sources. See Tilly (2005), p 85.

BIBLIOGRAPHY

Abbasi, Mustafa (2005). 'The "Aristocracy" of the Upper Galilee: Safad Notables and the Tanzimat Reforms', in *Ottoman Reform and Muslim Regeneration*, ed Itzchak Weismann and Fruma Zachs (London, New York: I.B.Tauris), pp 167–185

Abbott, Andrew (1997). 'On the Concept of Turning Point', *Comparative Social Research* 16, pp 85–105

Abdullah, Thabit A. J. (2000). *Merchants, Mamluks and Murder* (Albany: SUNY Press)

Abou-El-Haj, Rifa'at Ali (2005). *Formation of the Modern State – The Ottoman Empire, Sixteenth to Eighteenth Centuries* Second Edition (Syracuse: Syracuse University Press)

Abou-El-Haj, Rifa'at Ali (1982). 'The Social Uses of the Past: Recent Arab Historiography of Ottoman Rule', *International Journal of Middle East Studies* 14, 2, pp 185–201

Abu-Manneh, Butrus (2003). 'Salafiyya and the Rise of the Khalidiyya in Baghdad in Early Nineteenth Century', *Die Welt des Islams* 43, 3, pp 349–372

Abu-Manneh, Butrus (1998). 'The Genesis of Midhat Pasha's Governorship in Syria 1878–1880', in *The Syrian Land: Processes of Integration and Fragmentation: Bilad al-Sham from the 18th to the 20th Century*, ed Thomas Philipp and Birgit Schaebler (Stuttgart: Steiner), pp 251–268

Abu-Manneh, Butrus (1992). 'The Establishment and Dismantling of the Province of Syria, 1865–1888', in *Problems of the Modern Middle East in Historical Perspective*, ed John P. Spagnolo (Reading: Ithaca Press), pp 7–26

Abu-Maneh, Butrus (1980). 'The Christians between Ottomanism and Syrian Nationalism: the Ideas of Butrus Al-Bustani', *International Journal of Middle East Studies* 11, 3, pp 287–304

Adams, Julia (2005). *The Familial State: Ruling Families and Merchant Capitalism in Early Modern Europe* (Ithaca: Cornell University Press)

Adams, Julia, Elisabeth S. Clemens, and Ann Shola Orloff (eds) (2005). *Remaking Modernity: Politics, History and Sociology* (Durham: Duke University Press)

Adanır, Fikret (2001). *Makedonya Sorunu* (Istanbul: Tarih Vakfı Yayınları)

Adanır, Fikret (2000). 'Balkan Historiography related to the Ottoman Empire since 1945', in Ottoman Past and Today's Turkey, ed Kemal H. Karpat (Leiden: Brill), pp 236–252

Adelman, Jeremy (2006). *Sovereignty and Revolution in the Iberian Atlantic* (Princeton: Princeton University Press)

Agmon, Iris (2003). 'Text, Court and Family in Late-Nineteenth-Century Palestine', in *Family History in the Middle East: Household, Property and Gender*, ed Beshara Doumani (Albany: SUNY Press), pp 201–228

Ahmad, Feroz (2003). *Turkey: the Quest for Identity* (Oxford: Oneworld)

Ahmad, Feroz (2002). 'The Special Relationship: The Committtee of Union and Progress and the Jewish Political Elite, 1908–1918', in *Jews, Turks, Ottomans*, ed Avigdor Levy (Syracuse: Syracuse University Press), pp 212–230

Ahmad, Feroz (1988). 'War and Society under the Young Turks, 1908–1918', *Review* 11, 2, pp 265–286

Ahmad, Feroz (1980). 'Vanguard of a Nascent Bourgeoisie: the Social and Economic Policy of the Young Turks', in *Social and Economic History of Turkey*, ed Osman Okyar and Halil İnalcık (Ankara: Meteksan), pp 329–350

AHR Forum (2006). 'Oceans of History', *American Historical Review* 111, 3, pp 717–780

Akarlı, Engin Deniz (1993). *The Long Peace: Ottoman Lebanon, 1860–1920* (Berkeley: University of California Press)

Aktepe, M. Münir (1958). *Patrona İsyanı, 1730* (Istanbul: İ.Ü. Edebiyat Fakültesi)

Alkan, Mehmet Ö. (ed) (2004). *Tanzimat ve Meşrutiyet'in Birikimi Modern Türkiye'de Siyasi Düşünce* vol. 1 Sixth Edition (Istanbul: Iletişim)

Ali Bey (2003). *Dicle'de Kelek ile Yolculuk: Seyahat Jurnali (İstanbul'dan Bağdat'a ve Hindistan'a) Min Sene 1300 ile Sene 1304 (1884–1888)* (Istanbul: Büke Yayıncılık)

American Behavioral Scientist (2007). Special Issue 50, 8

Aminzade, Ron and Doug McAdam (2001). 'Emotions and Contentious Politics', in *Silence and Voice in the Study of Contentious Politics*, ed Ronald Aminzade et al. (Cambridge: Cambridge University Press), pp 14–50

Anderson, M. S. (1966). *The Eastern Question, 1774–1923: a Study in International Relations* (London: Macmillan)

Anscombe, Frederick F. (1997). *The Ottoman Gulf: the Creation of Kuwait, Saudi Arabia and Qatar* (New York: Columbia University Press)

Antonius, George (1938). *The Arab Awakening: the Story of the Arab National Movement* (London: H. Hamilton)

Aydın, Cemil (2007). *The Politics of anti-Westernism in Asia: Visions of World Order in Pan-Islamic and Pan-Asian Thought* (New York: Columbia University Press)

Baer, Marc David (2010). *The Dönme-Jewish Converts, Muslim Revolutionaries and Secular Turks* (Stanford: Stanford University Press)

Baldry, John (1976a). 'Anglo-Italian Rivalry in Yemen and Asir 1900–1934', *Die Welt des Islams* 17, 1–4, pp 155–193

Baldry, John (1976b). 'Al-Yaman and the Turkish Occupation, 1849–1914', *Arabica* 23, pp 156–196

Bang, Anne K. (1996). *The Idrisi State in Asir 1906–1934* (Bergen: University of Bergen)

Barkey, Karen (2008). *Empire of Difference- The Ottomans in Comparative Perspective* (Cambridge: Cambridge University Press)

Barkey, Karen (2005). 'A Perspective on Ottoman Decline', in *Hegemonic Decline: Present and Past*, ed Jonathan Friedman and Christopher Chase-Dunn (Boulder: Paradigm), pp 135–151

Barkey, Karen (1991). 'Rebellious Alliances: the State and Peasant Unrest in Early Seventeenth Century France and the Ottoman Empire', *American Sociological Review* 56, 6, pp 699–715

Bataru, Hanna (1978). *The Old Social Classes and the Revolutionary Movements of Iraq* (Princeton: Princeton University Press)

Bates, Robert H. (2001). *Prosperity and Violence: the Political Economy of Development* (New York: Norton)

Baud, Michiel and Willem van Schendel. 'Toward a Comparative History of Borderlands', *Journal of World History* 8, 2, pp 211–242

Beinin, Joel (2001). *Workers and Peasants in the Middle East* (Cambridge: Cambridge University Press)

Berkes, Niyazi (1964). *The Development of Secularism in Turkey* (Montreal: McGill University Press)

Birinci, Ali (1990). *Hürriyet ve İtilâf Fırkası: II. Meşrutiyet Devrinde İttihat ve Terakki'ye Karşı Çıkanlar* (Istanbul: Dergah)

Birtek, Faruk (2007). 'From Affiliation to Affinity: Citizenship in the Transition from Empire to the Nation-State', in *Identities, Affiliations, and Allegiances*, ed Seyla Benhabib, Ian Shapiro and Danilo Petranovic (Cambridge: Cambridge University Press), pp 17–44

Blok, Anton (1974). *The Mafia of a Sicilian Village, 1860–1960: a Study of Violent Peasant Entrepreneurs* (Oxford: Blackwell)

Bloxham, Donald (2005). *The Great Game of Genocide: Imperialism, Nationalism and the Destruction of Ottoman Armenians* (Oxford: Oxford University Press)

Blumi, Isa (2003a). 'Thwarting the Ottoman Empire: Smuggling through the Empire's New Frontiers in Yemen and Albania, 1878–1910', *International Journal of Turkish Studies* 9, 1, pp 255–274

Blumi, Isa (2003b). 'Beyond the Margins of the Empire: Searching the Limitations of Ottoman Rule in Yemen and Albania', *The MIT Electronic Journal of Middle East Studies* 3 (Spring), pp 18–26

Bozarslan, M. Emin (ed) (1991). *Kurdistan (1898–1902)* vol 2 (Uppsala: Deng)

Brower, Daniel R. and Edward J. Lazzerini (eds) (1997). *Russia's Orient: Imperial Borderlands and Peoples, 1700–1917* (Bloomington: Indiana University Press)

Brown, L. Carl (ed) (1996). *Imperial Legacy: the Ottoman Imprint in the Balkans and the Middle East* (New York: Columbia University Press)

Bruinessen, Martin van (1992). *Agha, Shaikh and State – The Social and Political Structures of Kurdistan* (London: Zed Books)

Brustein, William and Margaret Levi (1987). 'The Geography of Rebellion: Rulers, Rebels and Regions, 1500–1700', *Theory and Society* 16, 4, pp 467–495

Bryant, Joseph M. (2006). 'The West and the Revisited: Debating Capitalist Origins, European Colonialism and the Advent of Modernity', *The Canadian Journal of Sociology* 31, 4, pp 403–444

Buheiry, Marwan R. (1981). 'The Agricultural Exports of Southern Palestine, 1885–1914', *Journal of Palestine Studies* 10, 4, pp 61–81

Burke, Edmund (1991). 'Changing Patterns of Protest in the Middle East, 1750–1950', in *Peasants and Politics in the Modern Middle East*, ed Farhad Kazemi and John Waterbury (Miami: Florida International University Press), pp 24–37

Burke, Peter (2005). *History and Social Theory*, Second Edition (Ithaca: Cornell University Press)

Çadırcı, Musa (1991). *Tanzimat Döneminde Anadolu Kentleri'nin Sosyal ve Ekonomik Yapıları* (Ankara: Türk Tarih Kurumu Basımevi)

Calhoun, Craig, Frederick Cooper and Kevin W. Moore (eds) (2006). *Lessons of Empire- Imperial Histories and American Power* (New York: New Press)

Campos, Michelle U. (2005). 'Between "Beloved Ottomania" and the "Land of Israel": the Struggle over Ottomanism and Zionism among Palestine's Sephardi Jews, 1908–1913', *International Journal of Middle East Studies* 37, pp 461–483

Çelik, Zeynep (1986). *The Re-making of Istanbul: Portrait of an Ottoman City in the Nineteenth Century* (Seattle: University of Washington Press)

Centeno, Miguel Angel (2002). *Blood and Debt: War and the Nation-State in Latin America* (University Park: Pennsylvania State University Press)

Centeno, Miguel Angel (1997). 'Blood and Debt: War and Taxation in Nineteenth Century Latin America', *American Journal of Sociology* 102, 6, pp 1565–1605

Çetinsaya, Gökhan (2006). *Ottoman Administration of Iraq, 1890–1908* (London: Routledge)

Çetinsaya, Gökhan (2005). 'The Caliph and the Shaykhs: Abdülhamid II's Policy towards the Qaditiyya of Mosul', in *Ottoman Reform and Muslim Regeneration*, ed Itzchak Weismann and Fruma Zachs (London, New York: I.B.Tauris), pp 97–107

Çetinsaya, Gökhan (2003). 'The Ottoman View of British Presence in Iraq and the Gulf: the Era of Abdulhamid II', *Middle Eastern Studies* 39, 2, pp 194–203

Chalcraft, John T. (2004). *The Striking Cabbies of Cairo and other Stories: Crafts and Guilds in Egypt, 1863–1914* (Albany: SUNY Press)

Chalcraft, John (2002). 'The Cairo Cab Drivers and the Strike of 1907', in *The Empire in the City- Arab Provincial Capitals in the Late Ottoman Empire*, ed Jens Hanssen, Thomas Philipp and Stefan Weber (Beirut: Orient Institute), pp 173–198

Clay, Christopher (1998). 'Labour Migration and Economic Conditions in Nineteenth-Century Anatolia', *Middle Eastern Studies* 34, 4, pp 1–32

Clay, Christopher (1994). 'The Origins of Modern Banking in the Levant: the Branch Network of the Ottoman Imperial Bank, 1890–1914', *International Journal of Middle East Studies* 26, 4, pp 589–614

Clemens, Elisabeth S. and James M. Cook (1999). 'Politics and Institutionalism: Explaining Durability and Change', *Annual Review of Sociology* 25, pp 441–466

Cleveland, William L. (1978). 'The Municipal Council of Tunis, 1858–1870: A Study of Urban Institutional Change', *International Journal of Middle East Studies* 9, 1, pp 33–61

Cook, Karen S., Russell Hardin and Margaret Levi (2005). *Cooperation without Trust ?* (New York: Russell Sage Foundation)

Cooley, Alexander (2005). *Logics of Hierarchy: the Organization of Empire, States and Military Occupations* (Ithaca: Cornell University Press)

Cooper, Frederick (2006). 'Modernizing Colonialism and the Limits of Empire', in *Lessons of Empire- Imperial Histories and American Power*, ed Craig Calhoun, Frederick Cooper and Kevin W. Moore (New York: the New Press), 63–72

Cooper, Frederick (2005). *Colonialism in Question: Theory, Knowledge and History* (Berkeley: University of California Press)

Cooper, Frederick (2002). 'Decolonizing Situations: the Rise, Fall and Rise of Colonial Studies, 1951–2001', *French Politics, Culture and Society* 20, 2, pp 47–76

Crouch, Colin and Henry Farrell (2004). 'Breaking the Path of Institutional Development? Alternatives to the New Determinism', *Rationality & Society* 16, 1, pp 5–43

Curtin, Philip D. (2000). *The World and the West –The European Challenge in the Age of Empire* (Cambridge: Cambridge University Press)

Curtin, Philip D. (1999). 'Location in History: Argentina and South Africa in the Nineteenth Century', *Journal of World History* 10, 1, pp 41–92

Dasnabedian, Hratch (1990). *History of the Armenian Revolutionary Federation Dashnaksutiun 1890–1924* (Milan: Oemme Edizioni)

Davison, Roderic H. (1990). *Essays in Ottoman and Turkish History, 1774–1923: the Impact of the West* (Austin: University of Texas Press)

Davison, Roderic H. (1963). *Reform in the Ottoman Empire, 1856–1876* (Princeton: Princeton University Press)

Dawn, C. Ernest (1973). *From Ottomanism to Arabism: Essays on the Origins of Arab Nationalism* (Urbana: University of Illinois Press)

Deringil, Selim (2003). 'They Live in a State of Nomadism and Savagery: the Late Ottoman Empire and the Post-Colonial Debate', *Comparative Studies in Society and History* 45, 2, pp 311–342

Deringil, Selim (1998). *The Well-Protected Domains: Ideology and Legitimation of Power in the Ottoman Empire, 1876–1909* (London & New York: I.B.Tauris)

Deringil, Selim (1990). 'The Struggle Against Shiism in Hamidian Iraq: a Study in Ottoman Counter-Propaganda', *Die Welt des Islams* 30, 1–4, pp 45–62

Doumani, Beshara (2003). 'Adjudicating Family: The Islamic Courts and Disputes Between Kin in Greater Syria, 1700–1860', in *Family History in the Middle East*, ed Beshara Doumani (Albany: SUNY Press), pp 173–200

Doumani, Beshara (1998). 'Endowing Family: Waqf, Property Devolution and Gender in Greater Syria, 1800–1860', *Comparative Studies in History and Society* 40, 1, pp 3–41

Doumani, Beshara (1995). *Rediscovering Palestine: Merchants and Peasants in Jabal Nablus, 1700–1900* (Berkeley: University of California Press)

Duara, Prasenjit (1995). *Rescuing History from the Nation* (Chicago: University of Chicago Press)

Dumont, Paul (1999). 'Bir Osmanlı Sosyalizminin Doğuşu', in *Selanik 1850–1918*, ed Gilles Veinstein (Istanbul: İletişim), pp 205–217

Dural, Halil (1999). *19. ve 20. Yüzyılda Ege'de Efeler* (Istanbul: Tarih Vakfı Yurt Yayınları)

Emir Şekib Arslan (2008). *İttihatçı bir Arap Aydınının Anıları* (Istanbul: Klasik Yayınları)

Emrence, Cem (2006). *99 Günlük Muhalefet: Serbest Cumhuriyet Fırkası* (Istanbul: İletişim)

Emrence, Cem (1999). 'Alınan Koruyucu Önlemler ve Istanbul'da Kolera Salgını, 1893–1894', *Tarih ve Toplum* 32, 188, pp 46–52

Erickson, Edward J. (2001). *Ordered to Die: a History of the Ottoman Army in the First World War* (Westport: Greenwood Press)

Ertman, Thomas (1997). *The Birth of the Leviathan: Building States and Regimes in Medieval and Early Modern Europe* (Cambridge: Cambridge University Press)

Esherick, Joseph W., Hasan Kayalı and Eric Van Young (eds) (2006). *Empire to Nation* (Boulder: Rowman & Littlefield)

Esping-Andersen, Gosta (1990). *The Three Worlds of Capitalism* (Princeton: Princeton University Press)

Exertzoglou, Haris (2007). 'Metaphors of Change: "Tradition" and the East/West Discourse in the Late Ottoman Empire', in *Ways to Modernity in Greece and Turkey- Encounters with Europe, 1850–1950*, ed Anna Frangoudaki and Caglar Keyder (London: I.B.Tauris), pp 43–59

Exertzoglou, Haris (2003). 'The Cultural Uses of Consumption: Negotiating Class, Gender and Nation in the Ottoman Urban Centers during the 19th Century', *International Journal of Middle East Studies* 35, pp 77–101

Exertzoglou, Haris (1999). 'The Development of a Greek Ottoman Bourgeoisie: Investment Patterns in the Ottoman Empire, 1850–1914', in *Ottoman Greeks in the Age of Nationalism*, ed Dimitri Gondicas and Charles Issawi (Princeton: The Darwin Press), pp 89–114

Farah, Caesar (2002). *The Sultan's Yemen: Nineteenth Century Challenges to Ottoman Rule* (London: I.B.Tauris)

Farah, Caesar F. (1986). 'Protestanism and Politics: The 19th Century Dimension in Syria', in *Palestine in the Late Ottoman Period*, ed David Kushner (Leiden: E.J. Brill), pp 320–340

Faroqhi, Suraiya (2009). *Artisans of Empire- Crafts and Craftspeople under the Ottomans* (London: I.B.Tauris)

Faroqhi, Suraiya (ed) (2006). *The Cambridge History of Turkey Vol. 3 –The Later Ottoman Empire, 1603–1839* (New York: Cambridge University Press)

Faroqhi, Suraiya (1999). *Approaching Ottoman History: an Introduction to Sources* (New York: Cambridge University Press)

Faroqhi, Suraiya (1991a). 'Wealth and Power in the Land of Olives: Economic and Political Activities of Müridzade Hacı Mehmed Agha, Notable of Edremit', in *Landholding and Commercial Agriculture in the Middle East*, ed Çağlar Keyder and Faruk Tabak (Albany: SUNY Press), pp 77–95

Faroqhi, Suraiya (1991b). 'Introduction', *New Perspectives on Turkey* 5–6, pp 1–27

Farouk-Sluglett, Marion and Peter Sluglett (1991). 'The Historiography of Modern Iraq', *The American Historical Review* 96, 5, pp 1408–1421

Farouk-Sluglett, Marion and Peter Sluglett (1983). 'The Transformation of Land Tenure and Rural Social Structure in Central and Southern Iraq, c. 1870–1958', *International Journal of Middle East Studies* 15, 4, pp 491–505

Fattah, Hala (1997). *The Politics of Regional Trade in Iraq, Arabia and the Gulf, 1745–1900* (Albany: SUNY Press)

Fattah, Hala (1991). 'The Politics of Grain Trade in Iraq, c. 1840–1917', *New Perspectives on Turkey* 5–6, pp 151–166

Fawaz, Leila (1998). 'The Beirut-Damascus Road: Connecting the Syrian Coast to the Interior in the 19th Century', in *The Syrian Land:Processes of Integration and Fragmentation: Bilad al-Sham from the 18th to the 20th Century*, ed Thomas Philipp and Birgit Schaebler (Stuttgart: Steiner), pp 19–27

Fawaz, Leila Tarazi (1983). *Merchants and Migrants in Nineteenth Century Beirut* (Cambridge: Harvard University Press)

Fearon, James D. and David D. Laitin (2003). 'Ethnicity, Insurgency and Civil War', *American Political Science Review* 9, 1, pp 75–90

Ferguson, Niall (2003). *Empire- The Rise and Demise of the British World Order and the Lessons for Global Power* (New York: Basic Books)

Findley, Carter V. (1989). *Ottoman Civil Officialdom: a Social History* (Princeton: Princeton University Press)

Findley, Carter V. (1980). *Bureaucratic Reform in the Ottoman Empire* (Princeton: Princeton University Press)

Firro, Kais M. (2005). 'The Ottoman Reform and Jabal al-Duruz, 1860–1914', in *Ottoman Reform and Muslim Regeneration*, ed Itzchak Weismann and Fruma Zachs (London, New York: I.B.Tauris), pp 149–164

Firro, Kais M. (2003). *Inventing Lebanon – Nationalism and the State under Mandate* (London: I.B.Tauris)

Firro, Kais M. (1992). *A History of the Druzes* (Leiden, New York: E. J. Brill)

Firro, Kais (1990). 'Silk and Agrarian Changes in Lebanon, 1860–1914', *International Journal of Middle East Studies* 22, 2, pp 151–169

Foggo, Hacer Yıldırım (2002). *Kırmızı Püskül, 1843–1846 Nesturi Katliamı* (Istanbul: Çiviyazıları Yayınları)

Fortna, Benjamin C. (2008). 'The Reign of Abdülhamid II', in *The Cambridge History of Turkey* vol 4, ed Reşat Kasaba (Cambridge: Cambridge University Press), pp 38–61

Fortna, Benjamin C. (2002). *Imperial Classroom: Islam, Education and the State in the Late Ottoman Empire* (Oxford: Oxford University Press)

Frangakis-Syrett, Elena (1999). 'The Economic Activities of the Greek Community of Izmir in the Second Half of the Nineteenth and Early Twentieth Centuries', in *Ottoman Greeks in the Age of Nationalism*, ed Dimitri Gondicas and Charles Issawi (Princeton: The Darwin Press), pp 17–44

Frangakis-Syrett, Elena (1992). *The Commerce of Smyrna in the Eighteenth Century: 1700–1820* (Athens: Centre for Asia Minor Studies)

Fuccaro, Nelida (2003). 'Kurds and Kurdish Nationalism in Mandatory Syria: Politics, Culture and Identity', in *Essays on the Origins of Kurdish Nationalism*, ed Abbas Vali (Costa Mesa: Mazda Publishers), pp 191–217

Fuccaro, Nelida (1999). 'Communalism and the State in Iraq: the Yazidi Kurds, c. 1869–1940', *Middle Eastern Studies* 35, 2, pp 1–26

Fuhrmann, Malte (2003). 'Cosmopolitan Imperialists and the Ottoman Port Cities-Conflicting Logics in the Urban Social Fabric', *Cahiers de la Méditerranée* 67, pp 150–163

Gellner, Ernest (1981). *Muslim Society* (Cambridge: Cambridge University Press)

Gelvin, James L. (1998). *Divided Loyalties: Nationalism and Mass Politics in Syria at the Close of Empire* (Berkeley: University of California Press)

Genç, Mehmet (2000). *Osmanlı İmparatorluğu'nda Devlet ve Ekonomi* (Istanbul: Ötüken)

Gerber, Haim (1987). *Social Origins of the Modern Middle East* (Boulder: L. Rienner)

Gieryn, Thomas F. (2000). 'A Space for Place in Sociology', *Annual Review of Sociology* 26, pp 463–496

Gilbar, Gad G. (2003). 'The Muslim Big Merchant-Entrepreneurs of the Middle East, 1860–1914', *Die Welt des Islams* 43, 1, pp 1–36

Gilbar, Gad G. (1998). 'Economic and Social Consequences of the Opening of New Markets: the Case of Nablus, 1870–1914', in *The Syrian*

Land: Processes of Integration and Fragmentation: Bilad al-Sham from the 18th to the 20th Century, ed Thomas Philipp and Birgit Schaebler (Stuttgart: Steiner), pp 281–292

Goldstone, Jack A. (2001). 'Toward a Fourth Generation of Revolutionary Theory', *Annual Review of Political Science* 4, pp 139–187

Goldstone, Jack A. and Charles Tilly (2001). 'Threat (and Opportunity): Popular Action and State Response in the Dynamics of Contentious Action', in *Silence and Voice in the Study of Contentious Politics*, ed Ronald Aminzade et al. (Cambridge: Cambridge University Press), pp 179–194

Gorski, Philip S. (1993). 'The Protestant Ethic Revisited: Disciplinary Revolution and State Formation in Holland and Prussia', *American Journal of Sociology* 99, 2, pp 265–316

Gould, Andrew G. (1976). 'Lords or Bandits? The Derebeys of Cilicia', *International Journal of Middle East Studies* 7, 4, pp 485–506

Gould, Roger V. (1996). 'Patron-Client Ties, State Centralization and the Whiskey Rebellion', *The American Journal of Sociology* 102, 2, pp 400–429

Gould, Roger V. (1995). *Insurgent Identities: Class, Community and Protest in Paris from 1848 to the Commune* (Chicago: University of Chicago Press)

Gould, Roger V. and Roberto M. Fernandez (1989). 'Structures of Mediation: a Formal Approach to Brokerage in Transaction Networks', *Sociological Methodology* 19, pp 89–126

Gounaris, Basil C. (1993). 'Salonica', *Review* 16, 4, pp 499–518

Granovetter, Mark (1985). 'Economic Action and Social Structure: the Problem of Embeddedness', *The American Journal of Sociology* 91, 3, pp 481–510

Great Britain. Foreign Office (1920). *Armenia and Kurdistan* (London: H. M. Stationary Office)

Greene, Molly (2005). 'The Ottoman Experience', *Daedelus* 134, 2, pp 88–99

Grehan, James (2007). *Everyday Life and Consumer Culture in 18th Century Damascus* (Seattle: University of Washington Press)

Grehan, James (2003). 'Street Violence and Social Imagination in Late Mamluk and Ottoman Damascus (ca. 1500–1800)', *International Journal of Middle East Studies* 35, pp 215–236

Greif, Avner (2006). *Institutions and the Path to the Modern Economy* (Cambridge: Cambridge University Press)

Greif, Avner and David D. Laitin (2004). 'A Theory of Endogenous Institutional Change', *The American Political Science Review* 98, 4, pp 633–652

Gülsoy, Ufuk (1994). *Hicaz Demiryolu* (Istanbul: Eren)
Günay, Nejla (2007). *Maraş'ta Ermeniler ve Zeytun İsyanları* (Istanbul: IQ Yayıncılık)
Haddad, Mahmoud (1998). 'The City, the Coast, the Mountain and the Hinterland: Beirut's Commercial Rivalries in the 19th and Early 20th Century', in *The Syrian Land:Processes of Integration and Fragmentation: Bilad al-Sham from the 18th to the 20th Century*, ed Thomas Philipp and Birgit Schaebler (Stuttgart: Steiner), pp 129–153
Haj, Samira (1997). *The Making of Iraq, 1900–1963: Capital, Power and Ideology* (Albany: SUNY Press)
Hakan, Sinan (2007). *Osmanlı Arşiv Belgelerinde Kürtler ve Kürt Direnişleri (1817–1867)* (Istanbul: Doz Yayınları)
Hanioğlu, M. Şükrü (2008a). 'The Second Constitutional Period, 1908–1918', in *The Cambridge History of Turkey* vol. 4, ed Reşat Kasaba (Cambridge: Cambridge University Press), pp 62–112
Hanioğlu, M. Şükrü (2008b). *A Brief History of the Late Ottoman Empire* (Princeton: Princeton University Press)
Hanssen, Jens (2005). *Fin de Siécle Beirut: the Making of an Ottoman Provincial Capital* (Oxford: Clarendon Press)
Hanssen, Jens (2004). 'From Social Status to Intellectual Activity: Some Prosopographical Observations on the Municipal Council in Beirut, 1868–1908', in *From the Syrian Land to the States of Syria and Lebanon*, ed Thomas Philipp and Christoph Schumann (Beirut: Orient Institute), pp 59–76
Harel, Yaron (1998). 'Jewish-Christian Relations in Aleppo as Background for the Jewish Response to the Events of October 1850', *International Journal of Middle East Studies* 30, 1, pp 77–96
Herzog, Christoph (2003) 'Corruption and the Limits of the State in the Ottoman Province of Baghdad during the Tanzimat', *The MIT Electronic Journal of Middle East Studies* 3 (Spring), pp 36–43
Herzog, Christoph (2002). 'Nineteeenth-Century Baghdad through Ottoman Eyes', in *The Empire in the City- Arab Provincial Capitals in the Late Ottoman Empire*, ed Jens Hanssen, Thomas Philipp and Stefan Weber (Beirut: Orient Institute), pp 311–328
Hirschon, Renee (ed) (2003). *Crossing the Aegean: an Appraisal of the 1923 Compulsory Population Exchange between Greece and Turkey* (New York: Berghahn Books)
Holt, P. M. and M.W. Daly (2000). *A History of the Sudan* Fifth Edition (New York: Longman)

Horden, Peregrine and Nicholas Purcell (2006). 'The Mediterranean and the New Thalassology', AHR Forum, *The American Historical Review* 111, 3, pp 722–74

Horowitz, Richard S. (2005). 'International Law and State Transformation in China, Siam and the Ottoman Empire during the Nineteenth Century', *Journal of World History* 15, 4, pp 445–486

Hourani, Albert (1968). 'Ottoman Reform and Politics of Notables', in *Beginnings of Modernization in the Middle East: the Nineteenth Century*, ed W. R. Polk and R. L. Chambers (Chicago: University of Chicago Press, pp 41–68

Hourani, Albert (1962). *Arabic Thought in the Liberal Age, 1798–1939* (London, New York: Oxford University Press)

Hudson, Leila (2008). *Transforming Damascus: Space and Modernity in an Islamic City* (London: I.B.Tauris)

İnalcık, Halil and Mehmet Seyitdanlıoğlu (eds) (2006). *Tanzimat: Değişim Sürecinde Osmanlı İmparatorluğu* (Ankara: Phoenix Yayınevi)

Ingram, Paul and Karen Clay (2000). 'The Choice-Within-Constraints New Institutionalism and Implications for Sociology', *Annual Review of Sociology* 26, pp 525–546

International Journal of Turkish Studies (2003). 9, 1

İslamoğlu, Huri and Peter C. Perdue (2009). 'Introduction', in *Shared Histories of Modernity-China, India and the Ottoman Empire*, ed Huri İslamoğlu and Peter C. Perdue (New Delhi: Routlege), pp 1–20

İslamoğlu, Huri (ed) (2004). *Constituting Modernity: Private Property in the East and West* (London, New York: I.B.Tauris)

İslamoğlu-İnan, Huricihan (ed) (1987). *The Ottoman Empire and the World-Economy* (Cambridge: Cambridge University Press)

Issawi, Charles (1999). 'Introduction', in *Ottoman Greeks in the Age of Nationalism*, ed Dimitri Gondicas and Charles Issawi (Princeton: The Darwin Press), pp 1–16

Issawi, Charles (1977). 'British Trade and Rise of Beirut, 1830–1860', *International Journal of Middle East Studies* 8, 1, pp 91–101

Jacobson, Abigail (2008). 'Negotiating Ottomanism in Times of War: Jerusalem during World War I through the Eyes of a Local Muslim Resident', *International Journal of Middle East Studies* 40, pp 69–88

Jwaideh, Albertine (1984). 'Aspects of Land Tenure and Social Change in Lower Iraq during Late Ottoman Times', in *Land Tenure and Social Transformation in the Middle East*, ed Tarif Khalidi (Beirut: American University of Beirut Press), pp 333–356

BIBLIOGRAPHY

Jwaideh, Albertine (1963). 'Midhat Pasha and the Land System of Lower Iraq', in *Middle Eastern Affairs* St. Antony's Papers no. 16, ed Albert Hourani (London: Chatto & Windus), pp 106–136

Jwaideh, Wadie (2006). *Kurdish Nationalist Movement- Its Origins and Development* (Syracuse: Syracuse University Press)

Kalaycıoğlu, Ersin and Ali Yaşar Sarıbay (eds) (1986). *Türk Siyasal Hayatının Gelişimi* (Istanbul: Beta)

Kansu, Aykut (1997). *The Revolution of 1908 in Turkey* (Leiden: E. J. Brill)

Karaca, Ali (1993). *Anadolu Islahatı ve Ahmet Şakir Paşa, 1838–1899* (Istanbul: Eren)

Karpat, Kemal H. (2001). *The Politicization of Islam: Reconstructing Identity, State, Faith and Community in the Late Ottoman State* (New York: Oxford University Press)

Karpat, Kemal H. (ed) (2000). *Ottoman Past and Today's Turkey* (Leiden: Brill)

Kasaba, Reşat (2006). 'Dreams of Empire, Dreams of Nations', in *Empire to Nation –Historical Perspectives om the Making of the Modern World*, ed Joseph W. Esherick, Hasan Kayalı, Eric Van Young (Lanham: Rowman & Littlefield), pp 198–225

Kasaba, Reşat (1994). 'A Time and a Place for the Non-State: Social Change in the Ottoman Empire during the 'Long Nineteenth Century', in *State Power and Social Forces*, ed Joel S. Migdal, Atul Kohli and Vivienne Shue (Cambridge: Cambridge University Press), pp 206–230

Kasaba, Reşat (1993). 'İzmir', *Review* 16, 4, pp 387–410

Kasaba, Reşat (1991). 'Migrant Labor in Western Anatolia, 1750–1850', in *Landholding and Commercial Agriculture in the Middle East*, ed Çağlar Keyder and Faruk Tabak (Albany: SUNY Press), pp 113–121

Kasaba, Reşat (1988). *The Ottoman Empire and the World Economy –The Nineteenth Century* (Albany: SUNY Press)

Kasaba, Reşat and Immanuel Wallerstein (1980). 'Incorporation into the World-Economy: Change in the Structure of the Ottoman Empire, 1750–1839' (Binghamton: Fernand Braudel Center)

Katznelson, Ira (1985). 'Working-Class Formation and the State: Nineteenth Century England in American Perspective', in *Bringing the State Back In*, ed Peter Evans, Dietrich Rueschemeyer and Theda Skocpol (Cambridge: Cambridge University Press), pp 257–284

Kayalı, Hasan (2008). 'The Struggle for Independence', in *The Cambridge History of Turkey* vol 4, ed Reşat Kasaba (Cambridge: Cambridge University Press), pp 112–146

Kayalı, Hasan (1997). *Arabs and Young Turks- Ottomanism, Arabism and Islamism in the Ottoman Empire, 1908–1918* (Berkeley: University of California Press)

Kayalı, Hasan (1995). 'Elections and the Electoral Process in the Ottoman Empire, 1876–1919', *International Journal of Middle East Studies* 27, pp 265–286

Keyder, Çağlar (1999). 'Peripheral Port-Cities and Politics on the Eve of the Great War', *New Perspectives on Turkey* 20 (Spring), pp 27–45

Keyder, Çağlar (1994). 'The Agrarian Background and the Origins of Turkish Bourgeoise', in *Developmentalism and Beyond: Society and Politics in Egypt and Turkey*, ed Ayşe Öncü, Çağlar Keyder and Saad Eddin Ibrahim (Cairo: The American University of Cairo Press), pp 44–74

Keyder, Çağlar and Faruk Tabak (eds) (1991). *Landholding and Commercial Agriculture in the Middle East* (Albany: SUNY Press)

Keyder, Çağlar (1991). 'Introduction: Large Scale Commercial Agriculture in the Ottoman Empire?', in *Landholding and Commercial Agriculture in the Middle East*, ed Çağlar Keyder and Faruk Tabak (Albany: SUNY Press), pp 1–16

Keyder, Çağlar (1988). 'Bureaucracy and Bourgeoisie: Reform and Revolution in the Age of Imperialism', *Review* 11, 2, pp 151–165

Keyder, Çağlar (1987). *State and Class in Turkey: a Study in Capitalist Development* (London: Verso)

Khalidi, Rashid (1997). 'The Formation of Palestinian Identity: the Critical Years, 1917–1923', in *Rethinking Nationalism in the Arab Middle East*, ed James Jankowski and Israel Gerschoni (New York: Columbia University Press, 1997), pp 171–190

Khalidi, Rashid (1991). 'Ottomanism and Arabism in Syria before 1914: A Reassessment', in *The Origins of Arab Nationalism*, ed Rashid Khalidi, Lisa Anderson, Muhammad Muslih, Reeva S. Simon (New York: Columbia University Press), pp 50–69

Khodarkovsky, Michael (2002). *Russia's Steppe Frontier: the Making of a Colonial Empire, 1500–1800* (Bloomington: Indiana University Press)

Khoury, Dina Rizk (2008). 'Political Relations between City and State in the Middle East, 1700–1850', in *The Urban Social History of the Middle East 1750–1950*, ed Peter Sluglett (Syracuse: Syracuse University Press), pp 67–103

Khoury, Dina Rizk (1991). 'The Introduction of Commercial Agriculture in the Province of Mosul and its Effects on the Peasantry, 1750–1850', in *Landholding and Commercial Agriculture in the Middle* East, ed Çağlar Keyder and Faruk Tabak (Albany: SUNY Press), pp 155–171

Khoury, Philip S. and Joseph Kostiner (eds) (1990) *Tribes and State Formation in the Middle East* (Berkeley: University of California Press)

Khoury, Philip S. (1987). *Syria and the French Mandate: the Politics of Arab Nationalism, 1920–1945* (Princeton: Princeton University Press)

Khoury, Philip S. (1983). *Urban Notables and Arab Nationalism: the Politics of Damascus, 1860–1920* (Cambridge: Cambridge University Press)

Khuri-Makdisi, Ilham (2003). 'Levantine Trajectories: the Formulation and Dissemination of Radical Ideals in and between Beirut, Cairo and Alexandria, 1860–1914', Unpublished Ph.D. Dissertation Harvard University

Kılıç, Mehmet Fırat (2006). 'Between Empires: the Movement of Sheikh Ubeydullah', *The International Journal of Kurdish Studies* 20, 1–2, pp 57–121

Kimeldorf, Howard (1988). *Reds or Rackets: the Making of Radical and Conservative Unions on the Waterfront* (Berkeley: University of California Press)

Kiser, Edgar (1999). 'Comparing Varieties of Agency Theory in Economics, Political Science and Sociology: an Illustration from State Policy Implementation', *Sociological Theory* 17, 2, pp 146–170

Klein, Janet (2002). 'Power in the Periphery: the Hamidiye Light Cavalry and the Struggle over Ottoman Kurdistan, 1890–1914', Unpublished Ph.D. Dissertation Princeton University

Köksal, Yonca (2002). 'Imperial Center and Local Groups: Tanzimatt Reforms in the Provinces of Edirne and Ankara', *New Perspectives on Turkey* (Fall), pp 107–138

Koliopoulos, John S. (1987). *Brigands with a Cause-Brigandage and Irredentism in Modern Greece, 1821–1912* (Oxford: Clarendon Press)

Koloğlu, Orhan (2003). *Osmanlı Meclislerinde Libya ve Libyalılar* (Istanbul: Boyut Yayın Grubu)

Kostiner, Joseph (1993). *The Making of Saudi Arabia, 1916–1936: from Chieftancy to Monarchical State* (New York: Oxford University Press)

Kramer, Gudrun (2008). 'Moving Out of Place: Minorities in Middle Eastern Urban Societies, 1800–1914', in *The Urban Social History of the Middle East, 1750–1950*, ed Peter Sluglett (Syracuse: Syracuse University Press), pp 182 223

Krasner, Stephen D. (1999). *Sovereignty-Organized Hypocrisy* (Princeton: Princeton University Press)

Kühn, Thomas (2002). 'Ordering Urban Space in Ottoman Yemen, 1872–1914', in *The Empire in the City- Arab Provincial Capitals in the Late Ottoman Empire*, ed Jens Hanssen, Thomas Philipp and Stefan Weber (Beirut: Orient Institute), pp 329–347

Kuran, Timur (2011). *The Long Divergence- How Islamic Law Held Back the Middle East* (Princeton: Princeton University Press)

Kurmuş, Orhan (1987). 'The Cotton Famine and its Effects on the Ottoman Empire', in *The Ottoman Empire and the World-Economy*, ed Huri İslamoğlu-İnan (Cambridge: Cambridge University Press), pp 160–169

Kurmuş, Orhan (1974). *Emperyalizmin Türkiye'ye Girişi* (Istanbul: Bilim Yayınları)
Kurşun, Zekeriya (1998). *Necid ve Ahsa'da Osmanlı Hakimiyeti* (Ankara: Türk Tarih Kurumu)
Kusher, David (1996). 'Ali Ekrem Bey, Governor of Jerusalem, 1906–1908', *International Journal of Middle East Studies* 28, 3, pp 349–362
Lapidus, Ira M. (1989). 'Muslim Cities as Plural Societies: the Politics of Intermediary Bodies', in *The Proceedings of International Conference on Urbanism in Islam* vol. 1 (Tokyo: Daisan-Shokan), pp 133–163
Leeuwen, Richard van (1991). 'Monastic Estates and Agricultural Transformation in Mount Lebanon in the 18th Century', *International Journal of Middle East Studies* 23, 4, pp 601–617
Levi, Margaret (1997). *Consent, Dissent and Patriotism* (New York: Cambridge University Press)
Levi, Margaret (1988). *Of Rule and Revenue* (Berkeley: University of California Press)
LeVine, A. Mark (2004). 'Land, Law and the Planning of Empire: Jaffa and Tel Aviv during the Late Ottoman and Mandate Periods', in *Constituting Modernity- Private Property in the East and West*, ed Huri İslamoğlu (London: I.B.Tauris), pp 100–146
Lewis, Bernard (2002). *What Went Wrong?:Western Impact and Middle Eastern Response* (New York: Oxford University Press)
Lewis, Bernard (1961). *The Emergence of Modern Turkey* (London: Oxford University Press)
Lewis, Geoffrey L. (1955). *Turkey* (New York: Praeger)
Lewis, Norman N. (1987). *Nomads and Settlers in Syria and Jordan, 1800–1980* (Cambridge: Cambridge University Press)
Lewy, Guenter (2005). *The Armenian Massacres in Ottoman Turkey: a Disputed Genocide* (Salt Lake City: University of Utah Press)
Lieberman, Victor B. (2003–2009). *Strange Parallels: Southeast Asia in Global Context, c. 800–1830* vols. 1–2 (Cambridge: Cambridge University Press)
Lieven, Dominic (2001). *Empire- The Russian Empire and Its Rivals* (New Haven: Yale University Press)
Lockman, Zachary (2004). *Contending Visions of the Middle East–The History and Politics of Orientalism* (Cambridge: Cambridge University Press)
Lockman, Zachary (1997). 'Arab Workers and Arab Nationalism in Palestine', in *Rethinking Nationalism in the Arab Middle East*, ed James Jankowski and Israel Gershoni (New York: Columbia University Press), pp 249–272
Longrigg, Stephen Hemsley (1925/1968). *Four Centuries of Modern Iraq* (Oxford: Clarendon Press)

Macauley, Melissa (2009). 'A World Made Simple: Law and Property in the Ottoman and Qing Empires', in *Shared Histories of Modernity-China, India and the Ottoman Empire*, ed Huri İslamoğlu and Peter C. Perdue (New Delhi: Routlege), pp 273–298

Mahoney, James (2004). 'Comparative-Historical Methodology', *Annual Review of Sociology* 30, pp 81–101

Mahoney, James and Dietrich Rueschemeyer (eds) (2003). *Comparative Historical Analysis in the Social Sciences* (New York: Cambridge University Press)

Mahoney, James (2001). *Legacies of Liberalism: Path Dependence and Political Regimes in Central America* (Baltimore: Johns Hopkins University Press)

Makdisi, Ussama (2008). *Artillery of Heaven: American Missionaries and the Failed Conversion of the Middle East* (Ithaca: Cornell University Press)

Makdisi, Ussama (2004). 'Rethinking American Missionaries and Nineteenth-Century Historiography of the Middle East', in *From the Syrian Land to the States of Syria and Lebanon*, ed Thomas Philipp and Christoph Schumann (Beirut: Orient Institute), pp 209–224

Makdisi, Ussama (2002a). 'Ottoman Orientalism', *American Historical Review* 107, 3, pp 768–796

Makdisi, Ussama (2002b). 'Rethinking Ottoman Imperialism: Modernity, Violence and the Cultural Logic of Ottoman Reform', in *The Empire in the City- Arab Provincial Capitals in the Late Ottoman Empire*, ed Jens Hanssen, Thomas Philipp and Stefan Weber (Beirut: Orient Institute), pp 29–48

Makdisi, Ussama (2000). *The Culture of Sectarianism: Community, History and Violence in Nineteenth-century Ottoman Lebanon* (Berkeley: University of California Press)

Malmisanij (2004). *Diyarbekirli Cemalpaşazadeler ve Kürt Milliyetçiliği* (Istanbul: Avesta)

Mandaville, Jon (1986). 'Memduh Pasha and Aziz Bey: Ottoman Experience in Yemen', in *Contemporary Yemen*, ed B. R. Pridham (London: Croom Helm), pp 20–33

Mann, Michael (2005). *The Dark Side of Democracy* (Cambridge: Cambridge University Press)

Mann, Michael (1986–1993). *The Sources of Social Power* vols. 1–2 (Cambridge: Cambridge University Press)

Ma'oz, Moshe (1968). *Ottoman Reform in Syria and Palestine, 1840–1861: the Impact of the Tanzimat on Politics and Society* (Oxford: Clarendon Press)

Mardin, Şerif (1997). 'The Ottoman Empire', in *After Empire:Multi-Ethnic Societies and Nation-Building: the Soviet Union and Russian, Ottoman and*

Habsburg Empires, ed Karen Barkey and Mark von Hagen (Boulder: Westview Press), pp 115–128

Mardin, Şerif (1974). 'Superwesternization in Urban Life in the Ottoman Empire in the Last Quarter of the 19th Century', in *Turkey: Geographical and Social Perspectives*, ed Peter Benedict and Erol Tümertekin (Leiden: Brill), pp 403–446

Mardin, Şerif (1973). 'Center-Periphery: a Key to Turkish Politics', *Deadalus* 102, pp 169–190

Mardin, Şerif (1962). *The Genesis of Young Ottoman Thought: a Study in the Modernization of Turkish Political Ideas* (Princeton: Princeton University Press)

Marufoğlu, Sinan (1998). *Osmanlı Döneminde Kuzey Irak, 1831–1914* (Istanbul: Eren)

Masters, Bruce (2001). *Christians and Jews in the Ottoman Arab World* (Cambridge: Cambridge University Press)

Masters, Bruce (1999). 'Aleppo: the Ottoman Empire's Caravan City', in *The Ottoman City between East and West*, ed Edhem Eldem, Daniel Goffman and Bruce Masters (Cambridge: Cambridge University Press), pp 17–78

Masters, Bruce (1992). 'The Sultan's Entrepreneurs: the Avrupa Tuccaris and Hayriye Tuccaris in Syria', *International Journal of Middle East Studies* 24, 4, pp 579–597

Masters, Bruce (1990). 'The 1850 Events in Aleppo: An Aftershock of Syria's Incorporation to the Capitalist World System', *International Journal of the Middle East Studies* 22, 1, pp 3–20

Masters, Bruce (1988). *The Origins of Western Economic Dominance in the Middle East* (New York: NYU Press)

Mazower, Mark (2005). *Salonica, The City of Ghosts* (New York: Alfred A. Knopf)

Mazower, Mark (1991). *Greece and the Interwar Economic Crisis* (Oxford: Clarendon Press)

McAdam, Doug, Sidney Tarrow and Charles Tilly (2001). *Dynamics of Contention* (Cambridge: Cambridge University Press)

McCarthy, Justin (1995). *Death and Exile: The Ethnic Cleansing of Ottoman Muslims 1821–1922* (Princeton: The Darwin Press)

McMichael, Philip (2000). *Development and Social Change* Second Edition (Thousand Oaks: Pine Forge Press)

Mentzel, Peter (2006). *Transportation Technology and Imperialism in the Ottoman Empire, 1800–1923* (Washington, D.C.: American Historical Association)

Metcalf, Thomas R. (2007). *Imperial Connections: India in the Indian Ocean Arena, 1860–1920* (Berkeley: University of California Press)

Mills, C. Wright (1956). *The Power Elite* (New York: Oxford University Press)
MIT Electronic Journal of Middle East Studies (2003). 3 (Spring)
Mitchell, Timothy (1988). *Colonising Egypt* (Cambridge: Cambridge University Press)
Molho, Rena (1992). 'Le Renouveau...', in *Salonique 1850–1918: La "ville des Juifs" et le réveil des Balkans*, ed Gilles Veinstein (Paris:Autrement), pp 64–78
Motyl, Alexander C. (2001). *Imperial Ends: the Decay,Collapse and Revival of Empires* (New York: Columbia University Press)
Muhammed Kürd Ali (2006). *Bir Osmanlı-Arap Gazetecinin Anıları* (Istanbul: Klasik Yayınları)
Nalbandian, Louise (1963). *The Armenian Revolutionary Movement* (Berkeley: University of California Press)
Nee, Victor and Richard Swedberg (eds) (2005). *The Economic Sociology of Capitalism* (Princeton: Princeton University Press)
New Perspectives on Turkey (1992). 'The 1838 Convention and Its Impact', Special Issue, 7 (Spring)
Nexon, Daniel H. and Thomas Wright (2007). 'What's at Stake in the American Empire Debate', *American Political Science Review* 101, 2, pp 253–271
North, Douglass C. (1990). *Institutions, Institutional Change and Economic Performance* (New York: Cambridge University Press)
Ocak, Ahmet Yaşar (2003). 'Islam in the Ottoman Empire: A Sociological Framework for a New Interpretation', *International Journal of Turkish Studies* 9, 1, pp 183–197
Ochsenwald, William (1984). *Religion, Society and the State in Arabia: the Hijaz under Ottoman Control, 1840–1913* (Columbus: Ohio State University Press)
Ochsenwald, William (1980). *The Hijaz Railroad* (Charlottesville: University Press of Virginia)
Ökçün, Gündüz A. (1997). *İktisat Tarihi Yazıları* (Ankara: Sermaye Piyasası Kurulu)
Ökçün, Gündüz A. (1971). *Osmanlı Sanayii -1913, 1915 Yılları Sanayi İstatistiki* (Ankara: Sevinç Matbaası)
Olson, Mancur (1993). 'Dictatorship, Democracy and Development', *The American Political Science Review* 87, 3, pp 567–576
Olson, Robert (1989). *The Emergence of Kurdish Nationalism and the Sheikh Said Rebellion, 1880–1925* (Austin: University of Texas Press)
O'Rouke, Kevin H. (1997). 'The European Grain Invasion, 1870–1913', *The Journal of Economic History* 57, 4, pp 775–801

Ortaylı, İlber (1983). *İmparatorluğun En Uzun Yüzyılı* (Istanbul: Hil)
Ostle, Robin (2002). 'Alexandria: A Mediterranean Cosmopolitan Center of Cultural Production', in *Modernity and Culture – From the Mediterranean to the Indian Ocean*, ed Leila Tarazi Fawaz and C.A. Bayly (New York: Columbia University Press), pp 314–329
Owen, Roger (ed) (2000). *New Perspectives on Property and Land on the Middle East* (Cambridge: Harvard University Press)
Owen, Roger (1987). 'The Silk-Reeling Industry of Mount Lebanon, 1840–1914: a Study of the Possibilities and Limitations of Factory Production in the Periphery', in *The Ottoman Empire and the World-Economy*, ed Huri İslamoğlu-İnan (Cambridge: Cambridge University Press), pp 271–283
Owen, Roger (1981). *The Middle East in the World Economy 1800–1914* (London: Methuen)
Özdemir, Bülent (2003). *Ottoman Reforms and Social Life: Reflections from Salonica, 1830–1850* (Istanbul: ISIS Press)
Özmucur, Süleyman and Şevket Pamuk (2002). 'Real Wages and Standards of Living in the Ottoman Empire, 1489–1914', *The Journal of Economic History* 62, 2, pp 293–321
Özoğlu, Hakan (2004). *Kurdish Notables and the Ottoman State: Evolving Identities, Competing Loyalties, and Shifting Boundaries* (Albany: SUNY Press)
Padgett, John F. and Christopher K. Ansell (1993). 'Robust Action and the Rise of the Medici', *The American Journal of Sociology* 98, 6, pp 1259–1319
Pagden, Anthony (2008). *Worlds at War- The 2,500 Year Struggle between East and West* (New York: Random House)
Pagden, Anthony (2005). 'Fellow Citizens and Imperial Subjects: Conquest and Sovereignty in Europe's Overseas Empires', *History & Theory* 44, 4, pp 28–46
Palairet, Michael (1997). *The Balkan Economies, c. 1800–1914* (New York: Cambridge University Press)
Pamuk, Şevket (2008). *Osmanlı'dan Cumhuriyete Küreselleşme, İktisat Politikaları ve Büyüme* Seçme Eserleri II (Istanbul: Türkiye İş Bankası Yayınları)
Pamuk, Şevket (2007). *Osmanlı Ekonomisi ve Kurumları* Seçme Eserleri I (Istanbul: Türkiye İş Bankası Kültür Yayınları)
Pamuk, Şevket (2006a). 'Estimating Economic Growth in the Middle East since 1820', *The Journal of Economic History* 66, 3, pp 809–828
Pamuk, Şevket (2006b). 'From Debasement to External Borrowing: Changing Forms of Deficit Finance in the Ottoman Empire, 1750–1914', in *Monetary and Fiscal Policies in South-East Europe-Historical and*

Comparative Perspectives, ed Şevket Pamuk and Roumen Avramov (Sofia: Bulgarian National Bank), pp 7–22

Pamuk, Şevket (2005). 'The Ottoman Economy in World War I', in *The Economics of World War I*, ed Stephen Broadberry and Mark Harrison (Cambridge: Cambridge University Press), pp 112–36

Pamuk, Şevket (1992). 'Anatolia and Egypt during the Nineteenth Century: a Comparison of Foreign Trade and Foreign Invesment', *New Perspectives on Turkey* 7 (Spring), pp 37–55

Pamuk, Şevket (1987). *The Ottoman Empire and European Capitalism, 1820–1913: Trade, Investment and Production* (Cambridge: Cambridge University Press).

Pappé, Ilan (1997). 'From the "Politics of Notables" to the "Politics of Nationalism": The Husayni Family, 1840–1922', in *Middle Eastern Politics and Ideas*, ed Ilan Pappé and Moshe Ma'oz (London: I.B.Tauris), pp 163–207

Parvus Efendi (1977). *Türkiye'nin Mali Tutsaklığı* (Istanbul: May Yayınları)

Peters, B. Guy, Jon Pierre and Desmond S. King (2005). 'The Politics of Path Dependency: Political Conflict in Historical Institutionalism', *The Journal of Politics* 67, 4, pp 1275–1300

Philipp, Thomas (2002). 'Acre; the First Instance of Changing Times', in *The Empire in the City—Arab Provincial Capitals in the Late Ottoman Empire*, ed Jens Hanssen, Thomas Philipp and Stefan Weber (Beirut: Orient Institute), pp 77–92

Pierson, Paul (2000). 'Increasing Returns, Path-Dependence, and the Study of Politics', *The American Political Science Review* 94, 2, pp 251–267

Pomeranz, Kenneth (2000). *The Great Divergence: Europe, China and the Making of the Modern World Economy* (Princeton: Princeton University Press)

Provence, Michael (2005). *The Great Syrian Revolt and the Rise of Arab Nationalism* (Austin: University of Texas Press)

Quataert, Donald (2005). *The Ottoman Empire, 1700–1922* Second Edition (Cambridge: Cambridge University Press)

Quataert, Donald (2002). 'The Industrial Working Class of Salonica, 1850–1912', in *Jews, Turks and Ottomans*, ed Avigdor Levy (Syracuse: Syracuse University Press), pp 194–211

Quataert, Donald (1997). 'The Age of Reforms, 1812–1914', in *An Economic and Social History of the Ottoman Empire* vol. 2, ed Halil İnalcık and Donald Quataert (New York: Cambridge University Press), pp 761–943

Quataert, Donald and Erik Jan Zürcher (eds) (1995). *Workers and the Working Class in the Ottoman Empire and the Turkish Republic, 1839–1950* (London: I.B.Tauris)

Quataert, Donald (1995). 'The Workers of Salonica, 1850–1912', in *Workers and the Working Class in the Ottoman Empire and the Turkish Republic, 1839–1950*, ed Donald Quataert and Erik Jan Zürcher (London, New York: I.B.Tauris), pp 59–74

Quataert, Donald (1994a). 'Ottoman Manufacturing in the Nineteenth Century', in *Manufacturing in the Ottoman Empire and Turkey, 1500–1950*, ed Donald Quataert (Albany: SUNY Press), pp 87–121

Quataert, Donald (1994b). 'Ottoman Workers and the State, 1826–1914', in *Workers and Working Classes in the Middle East*, ed Zachary Lockman (Albany: SUNY Press), pp 21–40

Quataert, Donald (1993). *Ottoman Manufacturing in the Age of the Industrial Revolution* (Cambridge: Cambridge University Press).

Quataert, Donald (1991). 'Rural Unrest in the Ottoman Empire, 1830–1914', in *Peasants and Politics in the Modern Middle East*, ed Farhad Kazemi and John Waterbury (Miami: Florida International University Press), pp 38–49

Quataert, Donald (1988). 'Ottoman Handicrafts and Industry in the Age of Imperialism', *Review* 11, 2, 169–178

Quataert, Donald (1987). 'The Silk Industry of Bursa, 1880–1914', in *The Ottoman Empire and the World-Economy*, ed Huri İslamoğlu-İnan (Cambridge: Cambridge University Press), pp 284–308

Quataert, Donald (1983). *Social Disintegration and Popular Resistance in the Ottoman Empire, 1881–1908: Reactions to European Economic Penetration* (New York: NYU Press)

Quataert, Donald (1977). 'Limited Revolution: the Impact of the Anatolian Railway on Turkish Transport and the Provisioning of Istanbul, 1890–1908', *Business History Review* 51, 2, pp 139–160

Rafeq, Abdul-Karim (2000). 'Ownership of Real Property by Foreigners in Syria 1869 to 1873', in *New Perspectives on Property and Land in the Middle East*, ed Roger Owen (Cambridge: Harvard University Press), pp 175–239

Rafeq, Abdul-Karim (1988). 'New Light on the 1860 Riots in Ottoman Damascus', *Die Welt Des Islams* 28, 1–4, pp 412–430

Rafeq, Abdul-Karim (1984). 'Land Tenure Problems and their Social Impact in Syria', in *Land Tenure and Social Transformation in the Middle East*, ed Tarif Khalidi (Beirut: American University of Beirut Press), pp 371–396

Ragin, Charles C. (1987). *The Comparative Method: Moving Beyond Qualitative and Quantitative Strategies* (Berkeley: University of California Press)

Reilly, James (2002). *A Small Town in Syria: Ottoman Hama in the Eighteenth and Nineteenth Centuries* (Oxford, New York: P. Lang)

Reilly, James A. (1999). 'Past and Present in Local Histories of the Ottoman Period from Syria and Lebanon', *Middle Eastern Studies* 35, 1, pp 45–65

Reilly, James A. (1993). 'From Workshops to Sweatshops- Damascus Textiles and the World-Economy in the Last Ottoman Century', *Review* 16, 2, pp 199–213

Reilly, James A. (1992). 'Damascus Merchants and Trade in the Transition to Capitalism', *Canadian Journal of History* 27, 1, pp 1–27

Reilly, James A. (1989). 'Status Groups and Propertyholding in the Damascus Hinterland', *International Journal of Middle East Studies* 21, 4, pp 517–539

Reinkowski, Maurus (2003). 'Double Struggle, No Income: Ottoman Borderlands in Northern Albania', *International Journal of Turkish Studies* 9, 1, pp 239–253

Review (1993). 'Port-Cities of the Eastern Mediterranean, 1800–1914', Special Issue, 16, 4

Riasanovsky, Nicholas V. (1963). *A History of Russia* (New York: Oxford University Press)

Riley, Dylan (2005). 'Civic Associations and Authoritarian Regimes in Inter-War Europe: Italy and Spain in Comparative Perspective', *American Sociological Review* 70, 2, pp 288–310

Robinson, Richard D. (1965). *The First Turkish Republic* (Cambridge: Harvard University Press)

Roded, Ruth (1986). 'Social Patterns among the Urban Elite of Syria during the Late Ottoman Period, 1876–1918', in *Palestine in the Late Ottoman Period*, ed David Kushner (Leiden: E.J. Brill), pp 146–171

Rogan, Eugene L. (2004). 'The Political Significance of an Ottoman Education: Maktab 'Anbar Revisited', in *From the Syrian Land to the States of Syria and Lebanon*, ed Thomas Philipp and Christoph Schumann (Beirut: Orient Institute), pp 77–94

Rogan, Eugene L. (1999). *Frontiers of the State in Late Ottoman Empire: Transjordan 1850–1921* (Cambridge: Cambridge University Press)

Rogan, Eugene L. (1998). 'Instant Communication: The Impact of the Ottoman Telegraph in Ottoman Syria', in The Syrian Land: Processes of Integration and Fragmentation- Bilad al-Sham from the 18th to the 20th Century, ed Thomas Philipp and Birgit Schaebler (Stuttgart: Franz Steiner), pp 113–128

Rogan, Eugene L. (1996). 'Aşiret Mektebi: Abdulhamid II's School for Tribes (1892–1907)', *International Journal of Middle East Studies* 28, 1, pp 83–107

Rogan, Eugene L. (1994). 'Bringing the State Back: the Limits of Ottoman Rule in Transjordan, 1840–1910', in *Village, Steppe and State: the Social*

Origins of Modern Jordan, ed Eugene L. Rogan and Tariq Tell (London: British Academic Press), pp 32–57

Rogowski, Ronald (1989). *Commerce and Coalitions: How Trade Affects Domestic Political Alignments* (Princeton: Princeton University Press)

Rosenthal, Steven (1980). 'Foreigners and Municipal Reform in Istanbul 1855–1865', *International Journal of Middle East Studies* 11, pp 227–245

Salibi, Kamal (1988). *A House of Many Mansions- The History of Lebanon Reconsidered* (London: I.B.Tauris)

Salt, Jeremy (1993). *Imperialism, Evangelism and the Ottoman Armenians, 1878–1896* (London: Frank Cass)

Salzmann, Ariel (2004). *Tocqueville in the Ottoman Empire: Rival Paths to the Modern State* (Leiden: Brill)

Salzmann, Ariel (1999). 'Citizens in Search of a State: the Limits of Political Participation in the Ottoman Empire', in *Extending Citizenship, Reconfiguring States*, ed Michael Hanagan and Charles Tilly (Boulder: Rowman and Littlefield), pp 37–66

Salzmann, Ariel (1993). 'An Ancien Régime Revisited: "Privatization" and Political Economy in Eighteenth Century Ottoman Empire', *Politics & Society* 21, pp 393–423

Schaebler, Birgit (1998). 'State(s) Power and the Druzes: Integration and the Struggle for Social Control (1838–1949)', in *The Syrian Land: Processes of Integration and Fragmentation: Bilad al-Sham from the 18th to the 20th Century*, ed Thomas Philipp and Birgit Schaebler (Stuttgart: Steiner), pp 331–367

Schilcher, Linda Schatkowski (1991). 'The Great Depression (1873–1896) and the Rise of Syrian Arab Nationalism', *New Perspectives on Turkey*, 5–6, pp 167–189

Schilcher, Linda Schatkowski (1985). *Families in Politics: Damascene Factions and Estates in the 18th and 19th Centuries* (Stuttgart: Franz Steiner)

Schölch, Alexander (1984). 'The Decline of Local Power in Palestine after 1856: the Case of Aqil Aga', *Die Welt des Islams* 23, 1–4, pp 458–475

Schölch, Alexander (1981). 'The Economic Development of Palestine, 1856–1882', *Journal of Palestine Studies* 10, 3, pp 35–58

Seikaly, May (2002). 'Haifa at the Crossroads', in *Modernity and Culture – From the Mediterranean to the Indian Ocean*, ed Leila Tarazi Fawaz and C.A. Bayly (New York: Columbia University Press), pp 96–111

Seikaly, Samir (1991). 'Shukri al-'Asali: a Case Study of a Political Activist', in *The Origins of Arab Nationalism*, ed Rashid Khalidi, Lisa Anderson, Muhammad Muslih, Reeva S. Simon (New York: Columbia University Press), pp 73–96

Sewell, William (2005). *The Logics of History: Social Theory and Social Transformation* (Chicago: University of Chicago Press)

Shahvar, Soli. (2003). 'Tribes and Telegraphs in Lower Iraq: the Muntafiq and the Baghdad- Basrah Telegraph Line of 1863–65', *Middle Eastern Studies* 39, 1, pp 89–116

Shaw, Stanford J. (1978). 'The Ottoman System and Population, 1831–1914', *International Journal of Middle East Studies* 9, 3, pp 325–338

Shaw, Stanford J. and Ezel K. Shaw (1977). *History of the Ottoman Empire and Modern Turkey* vol. 2 (Cambridge: Cambridge University Press)

Shaw, Stanford J. (1975). 'The Nineteenth-Century Ottoman Tax Reforms and Revenue System', *International Journal of Middle Studies* 6, 4, pp 421–459

Shaw, Stanford J. (1971). *Between Old and New: the Ottoman Empire under Sultan Selim III, 1789–1807* (Cambridge: Harvard University Press)

Shields, Sarah (2000). *Mosul before Iraq: Like Bees Making Five-Sided Cells* (Albany: SUNY Press)

Shields, Sarah (1992). 'Mosul, the Free Trade Treaties, and the Lack of Impact on an Island Province', *New Perspectives on Turkey* 7, pp 113–123

Shields, Sarah (1991). 'Regional Trade and 19th Century Mosul: Revising the Role of Europe in the Middle East Economy', *International Journal of Middle East Studies* 23, 1, pp 19–37

Simon, Reeva S. (1991). 'The Education of an Iraqi Ottoman Army Officer', in *The Origins of Arab Nationalism*, ed Rashid Khalidi, Lisa Anderson, Muhammad Muslih, Reeva S. Simon (New York: Columbia University Press), pp 151–166

Sırma, İhsan Süreyya (1980). *Osmanlı Devleti'nin Yıkılışında Yemen İsyanları* (Istanbul: Zafer Matbaası)

Sluglett, Peter (2002). 'Aspects of Economy and Society in the Syrian Provinces: Aleppo in Transition, 1880–1925', in *Modernity and Culture – From the Mediterranean to the Indian Ocean*, ed L. T. Fawaz and C.A. Bayly (New York: Columbia University Press), pp 144–157

Snyder, Jack (1991). *Myths of Empire-Domestic Politics and International Ambition* (Ithaca: Cornell University Press)

Sonyel, Salahi R. (2000). *The Great War and the Tragedy of Anatolia: Turks and Armenians in the Maelstrom of Major Powers* (Ankara: Turkish Historical Society)

Spence, Jonathan D. (1990). *The Search for Modern China* (New York: Norton)

Stark, David and Laszlo Bruszt (1998). *Postsocialist Pathways: Transforming Politics and Property in East Central Europe* (Cambridge: Cambridge University Press)

Stinchcombe, Arthur L. (1997). 'On the Virtues of Old Institutionalism', *Annual Review of Sociology* 23, pp 1–18

Stoianovich, Trainan (1960). 'The Conquering Balkan Orthodox Merchant', *The Journal of Economic History* 20, 2, pp 234–313

Stoianovich, Trainan (1953). 'Land Tenure and Related Sectors of the Balkan Economy', *The Journal of Economic History* 13, 4, pp 398–411

Stoler, Ann Laura and Carole McGranahan (2007). 'Introduction: Refiguring Imperial Terrains', in *Imperial Formations*, ed Ann Laura Stoler, Carole McGranahan and Peter C. Perdue (Santa Fe: School for Advanced Research Press), pp 3–42

Stoler, Ann Laura, Carole McGranahan and Peter C. Perdue (eds) (2007). *Imperial Formations* (Santa Fe: School for Advanced Research Press)

Subrahmanyam, Sanjay (2006). 'A Tale of Three Empires- Mughals, Ottomans and Habsburgs in a Comparative Context', *Common Knowledge* 12, 1, pp 66–92

Sussnitzki, A. J. (1966). 'Zur Gliederung wirtschaftslicher Arbeit nach Nationalitaten in der Türkei', in *The Economic History of the Middle East 1800–1914*, ed Charles Issawi (Chicago and London: The University of Chicago Press), pp 114–125

Tabak, Faruk (2008). *The Waning of the Mediterranean, 1550–1870: a Geohistorical Approach* (Baltimore: Johns Hopkins University Press)

Tabak, Faruk (1988). 'Local Merchants in the Peripheral Areas of the Empire: the Fertile Crescent during the Long Nineteenth Century', *Review*, 11, 2, pp 179–214

Tekeli, İlhan and Selim İlkin (1989). *Ege'deki Sivil Direnişten Kurtuluş Savaşına Geçerken Uşak Heyet-i Merkeziyesi ve İbrahim (Tahtakılıç) Bey* (Ankara: Türk Tarih Kurumu Basımevi)

Tekeli, İlhan and Selim İlkin (1980). 'İttihat ve Terakki Hareketinin Oluşumunda Selanik'in Toplumsal Yapısının Belirleyiciliği', in *Social and Economic History of Turkey*, ed Halil İnalcık and Osman Okyar (Ankara: Meteksan), pp 351–82

Temin, Peter (2005). 'A Hobbessian Approach to Political-Economic History', *Journal of Interdisciplinary History* 35,4, pp 605–614

Terzibaşıoğlu, Yücel (2001). 'Landlords, Refugees and Nomads: Struggles for Land around Late Nineteenth Century Ayvalık', *New Perspectives on Turkey* 24, pp 51–82

Thelen, Kathleen (1999). 'Historical Institutionalism in Comparative Politics', *Annual Review of Political Science* 2, pp 369–404

Thompson, Elizabeth (1993). 'Ottoman Political Reform in the Provinces: the Damascus Advisory Council in 1844–45', *International Journal of Middle East Studies* 25, 3, pp 457–475

Thornton, Patricia H. (1999). 'The Sociology of Entrepreneurship', *Annual Review of Sociology* 25, pp 19–46

Tilly, Charles (2005). *Trust and Rule* (New York: Cambridge University Press)

Tilly, Charles (2001). 'Mechanisms in Political Processes', *Annual Review of Political Science* 4, pp 21–41

Tilly, Charles (1997). 'How Empires End', in *After Empire: Multiethnic Societies and Nation-Building: the Soviet Union, and Russian, Ottoman and Habsburg Empires*, ed Karen Barkey & Mark von Hagen (Boulder: Westview Press), pp 1–11

Tilly, Charles (1995). 'To Explain Political Processes', *The American Journal of Sociology* 100, 6, pp 1594–1610

Tilly, Charles (1990). *Coercion, Capital and European States, AD 990–1990* (Cambridge: Blackwell)

Tilly, Charles (1985). 'War-Making and State-Making as Organized Crime', in *Bringing the State Back In*, ed Peter B. Evans, Dietrich Rueschemeyer and Theda Skocpol (Cambridge: Cambridge University Press), pp 169–191

Toledano, Ehud R. (1997). 'The Emergence of Ottoman-Local Elites (1700–1900): A Framework for Research', in *Middle Eastern Politics and Ideas*, ed Ilan Pappé and Moshe Ma'oz (London: I.B.Tauris), pp 145–162

Toksöz, Meltem (2004). 'Ottoman Mersin: the Making of an Eastern Mediterranean Port-Town', *New Perspectives on Turkey* 31 (Fall), pp 71–89

Toprak, Zafer (2007). 'From Plurality to Unity: Codification and Jurisprudence in the Late Ottoman Empire', in *Ways to Modernity in Greece and Turkey-Encounters with Europe, 1850–1950*, ed Anna Frangoudaki and Caglar Keyder (London: I.B.Tauris), pp 26–39

Toprak, Zafer (1992). 'Modernization and Commercialization in the Tanzimat Period: 1838–1875', *New Perspectives on Turkey* 7, pp 57–70

Toprak, Zafer (1982). *Türkiye'de Milli İktisat, 1908–1918* (Ankara: Yurt Yayınları)

Turgay, A. Üner (1993). 'Trabzon', *Review* 16, 4, pp 435–465

Turgut, Ferdan (2002). 'Policing the Poor in the Late Ottoman Empire', *Middle Eastern Studies* 38, 2, pp 149–164

Vatter, Sherry (2006). 'Journeymen Textile Weavers in Nineteenth-Century Damascus: a Collective Biography', in *Struggle and Survival in the Modern Middle East*, ed Edmund Burke III and David N. Yaghoubian Second Edition (Berkeley: University of California Press), pp 64–79

Vatter, Sherry (1994). 'Militant Journeymen in Nineteenth-Century Damascus: Implications for the Middle Eastern Labor History Agenda', in *Workers and Working Classes in the Middle East*, ed Zachary Lockman (Albany: SUNY Press), pp 1–19

Vries, P.H.H. (2002). 'Governing Growth: A Comparative Analysis of the Role of State in the Rise of the West', *Journal of World History* 13, 1, pp 67–138

Watenpaugh, Keith David (2006). *Being Modern in the Middle East* (Princeton: Princeton University Press)

Watts, Duncan J. (2004). 'The "New" Science of Social Networks', *Annual Review of Sociology* 30, pp 243–270

Weber, Stefan (2004). 'Reshaping Damascus: Social Change and Patterns of Architecture in Late Ottoman Times', in *From the Syrian Land to the States of Syria and Lebanon*, ed Thomas Philipp and Christoph Schumann (Beirut: Orient Institute), pp 41–58

Weber, Stefan (2002). 'Images of Imagined World', in *The Empire in the City- Arab Provincial Capitals in the Late Ottoman Empire*, ed Jens Hanssen, Thomas Philipp and Stefan Weber (Beirut: Orient Institute), 145–171

Weismann, Itzchak (2001). *Taste of Modernity: Sufism, Salafiyya, and Arabism in late Ottoman Damascus* (Leiden: Brill)

Williamson, Jeoffrey G. (2002). 'Land, Labor and Globalization in the Third World, 1870–1940', *The Journal of Economic History* 61, 1, pp 55–85

Wilson, Mary C. (1987). *King Abdullah, Britain and the Making of Jordan* (Cambridge: Cambridge University Press)

Winter, Stefan. *The Shiites of Lebanon under Ottoman Rule, 1516–1788* (Cambridge: Cambridge University Press, 2010)

Wong, R. Bin (2006). 'China's Agrarian Empire: a Different Kind of Empire, a Different Kind of Lesson', in *Lessons of Empire- Imperial Histories and American Power*, ed Craig Calhoun, Frederick Cooper and Kevin W. Moore (New York: The New Press), pp 189–200

Wong, R. Bin (2001). 'Formal and Informal Mechanisms of Rule and Economic Development: the Qing Empire in Comparative Perspective', *Journal of Early Modern History* 5, 4, pp 387–408

Wong, Roy B. (1997). *China Transformed and the Limits of European Experience* (Ithaca: Cornell University Press)

Worringer, Renee (2004). '"Sick Man of Europe or Japan of the Near East"?: Constructing Ottoman Modernity in the Hamidan and Young Turk Eras', *International Journal of Middle East Studies* 36, 2, pp 207–230

Yazbak, Mahmoud (1998). 'Nablus versus Haifa, 1870–1914: Administrative Developments and their Impact on Social Stratification', in *The Syrian Land:Processes of Integration and Fragmentation: Bilad al-Sham from the 18th to the 20th Century*, ed Thomas Philipp and Birgit Schaebler (Stuttgart: Steiner), pp 269–279

Yazbak, Mahmoud (1998). *Haifa in the Late Ottoman Period, 1864–1914* (Leiden: Brill)

Yazbak, Mahmoud (1997). 'Nabulsi Ulama in the Late Ottoman Period, 1864–1914', *International Journal of Middle East Studies* 29, 1, pp 71–91

Yenişehirlioğlu, Filiz (2002). 'Mersin: the Formation of a Tanzimat City in Southern Turkey', in *The Empire in the City- Arab Provincial Capitals in the Late Ottoman Empire,* ed Jens Hanssen, Thomas Philipp and Stefan Weber (Beirut: Orient Institute), pp 253–274

Yıldırım, Onur (2006). *Diplomacy and Displacement: Reconsidering the Turco-Greek Exchange of Populations, 1922–1934* (New York: Routledge)

Yıldız, Hakkı Dursun (ed) (1992). *150. Yılında Tanzimat* (Ankara: Türk Tarih Kurumu Basımevi)

Yolalıcı, Emin M. (1998). *IX. Yüzyılda Canik (Samsun) Sancağının Sosyal ve Ekonomik Yapısı* (Ankara: Türk Tarih Kurumu Basımevi)

Zachs, Fruma (2005). *The Making of a Syrian Identity: Intellectuals and Merchants in Nineteenth Century Beirut* (Leiden: Brill)

Zachs, Fruma (2004). 'Building a Cultural Identity: the Case of Khalil al-Khuri', in *From the Syrian Land to the States of Syria and Lebanon,* ed Thomas Philipp and Christoph Schumann (Beirut: Orient Institute), pp 27–39

Zandi-Sayek, Sibel (2001). 'Orchestrating Difference, Performing Identity: Urban Space and Public Rituals in Nineteenth Century Izmir', in *Hybrid Urbanism,* ed Nezar AlSayyad (London: Praeger), pp 42–66

Zürcher, Erik Jan (2004). *Turkey: a Modern History* Third Edition (London: I.B.Tauris)

Zürcher, Erik Jan (1999). 'The Ottoman Conscription System in Theory and Practice', in *Arming the State- Military Conscription in the Middle East and Central Asia 1775–1925,* ed Erik J. Zürcher (London, New York: I.B.Tauris), pp 9–94

INDEX

Abbott, Andrew 3, 31
Abdulhamid II 18, 29, 81, 93, 103, 110, 129, 148
Acre 36, 39, 136
Adams, Julia 141
Adapazarı 112
Aden 87
Afyon 47, 149
Ahmad Izzat Paşa 59
Ahmad, Feroz 25, 133, 135, 148, 149
Ajlun 83, 89
al-Atrash Clan 83, 93, 119, 144, 145, 152
Albanians 125
Aleppo 39, 57, 65, 66, 68, 71, 89, 112, 114, 141, 142, 150, 154
   Jabirizade of Aleppo 59
   Mudarriszade of Aleppo 59
Al-Hafair 98
Ali Bey 143
Allatinis 38
Amanos Mountains 57
Aminzade, Ron 72, 143
Amir Shakib Arslan 108
Anatolia 4, 57, 66, 67, 73, 74, 102, 108, 109, 112, 127, 142
   Anatolian Railway 50, 66

Central Anatolia 13, 55, 57, 65, 66, 108, 110, 112
Eastern Anatolia 4, 11, 13, 24, 44, 75, 78, 80–82, 84–87, 89–98, 106, 115, 118, 119, 124, 130, 147, 148, 151, 152, 154
Southeastern Anatolia 65, 88, 98
Western Anatolia 4, 23, 29, 35–37, 41, 46, 107–109, 114, 120, 136, 138, 148
Anglo–Ottoman Trade Treaty 23
Ankara 60, 141, 154
Antep 66
Aqil Aga 56
Arabia
   Central Arabia 92
   Peninsula 4, 13, 75, 77, 83, 89, 97, 102, 116, 118, 119, 132, 146
   Rashidi of Arabia 95, 117, 119
Arabs 110, 126, 150
Armenian(s) 37, 44, 86, 87, 89, 92, 94, 115, 118, 140, 151
   Question 115
   Peasants 86, 93, 94, 115
   Revolutionaries 93, 148
artisan 6, 72, 73

Asir 78, 80, 83, 86, 87, 92, 96, 116, 117
Assyrians 125
Austria 106
autonomy 5–9, 12, 52, 63, 68, 75, 83, 90, 92–94, 98, 101, 102, 115, 116, 119–121, 123, 124, 126, 127, 129, 148, 149, 154
Ayvalık 48, 139

Bab Tuma 68
Baghdad 64–66, 85, 86, 89, 92, 119, 141, 143, 146
Balkan(s) 1, 11, 102, 106, 136, 138, 142
   Wars 107, 108, 116
   Balkanization 1
Balqa 83
Banque Imperiale Ottomane 38
Barkey, Karen 29, 135, 136, 152
Basra 83, 85, 87, 93, 116, 146
Bedirhan Bey of Botan 82, 147
Beirut 24, 39, 41–43, 49, 51, 107–109, 138, 148, 149
Berkes, Niyazi 20, 134
Berlin Congress 12, 94
Binghazi 78
Beqaa Valley 109
Black Sea 24, 39, 137
borderlands 75, 87, 124, 125, 130, 143, 148
Bosnia-Herzegovina 106
bourgeoisie 23, 26, 38, 41, 47, 50, 52, 138, 139
Britain 104, 125, 131, 145, 152
brokerage 85, 91, 123, 145
   religious 5, 90
Bruszt, Laszlo 3, 132
Bulgaria 24, 106, 135
bulk goods 39, 46, 63, 65–67, 73
Butrus El-Bustani 41

capitalism 3, 4, 10, 15, 22, 121
Caucasus 76, 118, 152–154
census 97, 127, 153

center–periphery 33, 68, 106, 128
   alliance 30
   conflict 20
   models 122
Central America 3
China 10
Çiftliks 24
citizenship 3, 76, 127, 153
civil society 13, 29, 52
clash of civilizations 1
coast 2, 4–10, 34–39, 41, 44–46, 50, 52, 65, 73–75, 83, 92, 99, 101, 106, 107, 109, 110, 120–124, 126, 127, 129, 132, 136–138, 149
coastal middle classes: 5, 41, 52, 101
Cold War 1, 11, 17, 124
collective action 5, 6, 9, 48, 52, 69, 90, 92, 93, 96, 98, 123, 124, 132, 139, 142, 152
collective claims 6, 67, 75, 90, 98, 121, 122
colonization 25
commercialization 3, 6, 36, 38, 39, 66, 67, 84
   cotton 36, 39, 65, 138
   olives 39
   oranges 39
   silk 36, 37, 39, 72, 136
   tobacco 24, 37–39, 48, 87
Committee of Union and Progress 25, 104–108, 110, 111, 112, 115, 148–151
communal 1, 5, 6, 8, 12, 30, 38, 45, 46, 48, 52, 68, 69, 91, 93, 95, 96, 98, 101, 109, 115, 120, 124, 127, 130, 138
   identity 42, 76, 94, 140
   tensions 46, 139
   ties 42
conflict path 12
conscription 58, 74, 93, 97, 127, 130, 153
contention 4–6, 31, 45, 46, 48, 52, 55, 69, 71, 73, 90, 101, 123, 129
   contentious politics 9, 72, 146

Index

cosmopolitan(ism) 5, 12, 44, 45, 106, 108, 124, 126, 129, 140
   actors 42, 49, 52, 66, 101, 107, 109, 120, 149
   rule 41, 126, 153
   space 44, 45, 153
Covenant Society (Ahd) 111
credit 37, 64, 107
Crete 106
Crimean War 23, 137
Çukurova Plain 39, 89, 139

Daman 64
Damascus 56, 57, 59, 62, 65, 68, 70, 72, 73, 89, 110, 112, 114, 129, 142, 150, 151, 154
decolonization 17
demography 75, 93, 108, 138, 146
   change 43, 44, 118
   expansion 38, 46, 48, 115
Dependency Approach 22–26
Deringil, Selim 29, 135, 143, 148
diplomatic history 15
Diyarbakır 29, 66, 86, 146, 147, 151, 152
dönme families 104, 148
Druze 46, 83, 84, 86, 89, 92, 95, 98, 107–109, 115, 137, 144, 145, 148, 153
   Jabal Druze 78, 89, 91, 93

Eastern Mediterranean 4, 8, 13, 35, 36, 39, 41, 44, 46, 48, 49, 52, 53, 108, 109, 122, 124, 126, 149
education 18, 30, 42, 60, 74, 78, 103, 104, 130, 151
Egypt 5, 56, 65, 68, 102, 111, 138, 146
Emir Faysal 112–114, 151
empire 1, 2, 4, 6, 9–13, 15, 17, 19, 29, 22–26, 29, 30, 32, 33, 35, 36, 38, 39, 41, 43, 52, 53, 55, 63, 66, 74, 81, 85, 97, 99, 101–106, 108, 110–112, 118, 119, 122, 124–130, 133, 135, 136, 139, 141, 143, 144, 148, 150, 153, 154

Ertman, Thomas 3, 131
Erzurum 73, 147
esnaf cemiyetleri 108, 149
Eurasia 1
Eurocentrism 27
Europe 3, 7, 23–26, 33, 36–39, 41, 42, 44, 49–51, 57, 67–69, 86, 103, 105, 107, 109, 119, 127, 131, 132, 134–139, 144, 148, 149, 153, 154
extra-territoriality 52, 132

family 29, 38, 57, 59, 60, 83, 87, 92–94, 118, 138, 140, 141, 147, 148, 151, 152
   Karaosmanoğulları Family 29
   Kozanoğulları Family 57
   Sadun Family of Basra 83, 87, 93
Faroqhi, Suraiya 65, 133, 136, 142
Fellah 88
frontier 4–10, 13, 30, 74–84, 86, 87, 90, 91, 95–99, 101–102, 104, 106, 115, 118–121, 123–125, 127, 129, 130, 133, 143, 144, 146, 152–154
   economy 87, 89, 90
   far frontier 8, 82–84, 86, 89, 92–94, 97, 98, 116, 119, 120, 127, 129, 146, 154
   leaderships 6, 8, 10, 63, 75, 78, 81, 90, 94, 95, 98, 101, 116, 118, 119, 147, 148
   intermediate frontier 93, 153
   mobilizations 90–92, 95, 98
   near frontier 82, 86, 89, 93–95, 98, 118, 119, 128, 129
   populations 57, 97, 119, 125
   vision 76, 151

Galilee 56
Gellner, Ernest 91, 146
geopolitics 77, 84, 143
   geopolitical competition 3, 4, 7, 12, 75, 97, 127, 145
Gieryn, Thomas 10, 133

global 2, 4, 7, 8, 15, 21, 22, 25, 26, 27, 31–33, 35, 36, 38, 42, 50–52, 55, 62, 74, 120, 122, 124, 126, 128, 131, 145, 154
  actors 7, 24, 36, 67
  flows 8, 27, 35, 41, 51, 121, 125, 126, 129
Gould, Andrew 95, 140, 147
governance 5, 43, 76, 133
  contested 6
  consensual 7, 55, 60
  indirect 16, 30, 95
  thin 6, 9, 13, 75, 83, 84, 90, 97, 123
grain 39, 46, 65, 89, 112
  belt 65
  merchants 46, 66, 67, 116, 142
great power politics 22
Greek(s) 36, 37, 48, 106–109, 125, 136, 138, 139, 149
  bourgeoisie 38, 139
  Greek Orthodox Church 106
Greene, Molly 74, 143
Grehan, James 73, 143
guild 25, 49, 67, 68, 72, 107, 108, 135, 139, 149
  organization 49
Gulf Region 83, 96

Haifa 39, 40, 48, 137, 139
Hama 57, 60, 65, 141
Hamidiye Cavalry 86, 94, 147
Hanioğlu, Şükrü 30, 136, 148
Hawran 39, 57, 65, 80, 83, 86, 89, 90, 92, 94, 96, 106, 129, 154
Hayderan Tribe 86
Herzog, Christoph 81, 143, 144
High Advisory Council of Damascus 59
Hijaz 80, 83, 85, 87, 96, 114, 117, 119, 145, 154
  Hijaz Railway 77, 116, 143
hinterland 4, 22, 36–39, 41, 44–47, 51, 52, 65, 101, 104, 107–109, 120, 123, 120, 138, 139, 149
historical trajectory 2, 5, 7, 8, 128

historiography 11, 13, 15–17, 21, 25–28, 30–34, 121, 133, 136, 148
Holy Sites 85, 86
Homs 65, 129
Hudayda 79, 146
Husaynis of Jerusalem 59

Ibrahim Hananu 114
ideology 3, 5, 6, 12, 19–21, 28, 30, 31, 41–43, 45, 52, 76, 79, 81, 92, 94, 95, 97, 103, 111, 112, 123, 125, 130, 134, 136, 145, 150
  cultural scripts 9
identity 1, 7, 11, 27, 29, 49, 60, 72, 74, 81, 91, 93, 96, 101, 105, 114, 122, 126, 140
Idrisi of Asir 83, 86, 87, 92, 98, 117
Ikhwan 119, 152
İlmiye 56, 140
Imperial-Arab Elite 112
imperialism 5, 23, 50, 75, 103, 125, 127, 135, 145
  European 23, 42, 144
  anti-imperialists 22, 25
  imperial paths 2, 4, 123
information 9, 37, 64, 81, 90, 91, 136, 144
institutionalism 9, 15,
  historical 8
  institutional economics 9
interior 2, 4–10, 53, 55–60, 62–69, 72–75, 78, 99, 101, 110–112, 114, 115, 120–127, 129, 130, 140, 146, 149, 150, 153
Iraq 1, 4, 13, 75, 77, 78, 80, 81, 84, 85, 88, 111, 114, 119, 125, 135, 144, 150, 153
  Central Iraq 87
  Lower Iraq 76, 82–85, 87, 93, 94, 96, 98, 116, 119
  Northern Iraq 64, 65, 82, 84, 86, 89, 90, 93, 96, 98, 112, 119, 141, 147, 154
Iskenderun 39

INDEX

189

Islam 9, 12, 18, 20, 29, 81, 92, 103, 106, 111, 116, 118, 119, 126, 130, 144, 146, 152
   Sunni 5, 7, 9, 57, 58, 75, 81, 92, 93, 97, 119, 125
   State 5, 62
   Heterodox 7, 9, 30, 92, 98
Issawi, Charles 23, 134, 136, 139
Istanbul 21, 39, 43–45, 49–51, 62, 66, 78–80, 82, 98, 106, 108, 112, 116, 118, 138, 140, 150, 151
Italy 3, 132
İttihad-ı Anasır 105
Izmir 36, 38, 42, 44, 47, 50, 51, 66, 107, 108, 129, 138–140, 149, 154

Jabal Amil 107
Jabal Sinjar 89
Jaffa 39, 48, 137, 139
Jews 37, 114, 115
Judayda 68

Kansu, Aykut 106, 148
Karak 83, 151, 154
Kars Treaty 118
Kasaba, Reşat 23, 134, 135, 138, 139
Kerkuk 89
kinship 37, 64, 91, 138, 141
Khalil al-Khuri 41
Khoury, Philip 59, 135, 141, 146, 152
Khuri-Makdisi, Ilham 43, 137, 138
Konya 65
Kosovo 11, 148
Kurd(s) 82, 86, 89, 91–95, 97, 118, 119, 125, 144, 145, 147, 150–152, 154
   Kurdish question 86
Kuwait 81, 87, 92, 116, 117
   Şeyh of Kuwait 81, 87

labor 23, 24, 57, 66, 67, 71–73, 86, 88, 132, 134, 135, 138, 143
Latin America 3, 132, 139, 153
landlord(ism) 36, 46, 57, 59, 60, 87, 98, 104, 107, 119,

Lebanon 30, 37, 46, 108, 109, 112, 136, 137, 150
   Greater Lebanon 108
   Lebanese Nahda Movement 42
   Mount Lebanon 37, 46, 107, 108, 127
Levant Army 115
Lewis, Bernard 17, 133
Liberal Entente 106, 148
Libya 78, 146
local elite 6, 28, 29, 31, 55, 56, 59, 60, 74, 83, 94, 97, 102, 143
   resources 60, 69, 83
   schemas 69

Ma'an 83, 85
Macedonia 11, 37, 46, 48, 94, 104, 108, 127, 139, 148
Mahmut II 17, 102
Mahoney, James 3, 131
Makdisi, Ussama 30, 135, 138, 140, 143
manufacturing 24, 37, 38, 63, 65–67, 71, 73, 89, 142
Maraş 68
Mardin 66
Mardin, Şerif 20, 134, 137
marriage 37, 60, 64, 83, 141
markets 5–7, 9, 10, 23, 36–39, 46, 50, 51, 55, 63, 65–69, 71–73, 75, 78, 85, 88–90, 98, 132, 137, 138, 142
   global 6, 23, 24, 46, 51, 52, 55, 109, 124, 150
   regional 6, 62, 63, 65–67, 69, 89, 98, 120, 123, 142
   towns 65, 129
Maronites 108
mass politics 13, 99, 101, 106, 111, 119, 149
mawat 64
McAdam, Doug 72, 132, 143
Mecca 81, 83, 86, 116, 117, 120, 127, 144, 151
   Sharif of Mecca 81, 83, 86, 116, 120, 127, 151
Medina 78, 85, 88, 116, 117

merchants 5, 6, 8, 22, 23, 29, 36–39, 41, 43–48, 50, 52, 56, 57, 63–69, 71–73, 87, 89, 97, 107, 108, 112, 122, 138, 140–142
Mersin 39, 65, 137
micro history 10, 15, 31
Midhat Paşa 84, 145
migration 44, 48, 88, 108, 109, 138
Milli Tribe 86
Miran Tribe 86
Mir Han Mahmud 82
Mir Muhammed of Soran 82
modernization 3, 8, 15–22, 27, 30, 32, 42, 43, 76–78, 121, 122, 133, 134, 140
Montenegro 87
Mosul 65, 68, 89, 119, 143
Motyl, Alexander 127, 153
Muhammad Abduh 111
Muhammad Ali Bey 59
Muhammad Ali of Egypt 102
Muhammadan Union 110
Mülkiye 61
municipal councils 5, 6, 43, 48, 52
Muntafiq Tribes 93
Muslim(s) 5, 6, 8, 9, 13, 29, 30, 36, 45–50, 55–57, 59, 60, 62–65, 67–69, 71, 74, 76, 93, 94, 97, 101, 104, 106–115, 118, 120, 123, 124, 126, 129, 138, 140–142, 148, 149
  privileges 68

Nablus 28, 56, 64, 65, 68, 69, 142
Nakşibendi 92, 97
  nakşibendi-khalidi sufi orders 94, 147
Napoleonic Wars 36
nation-state 1, 16, 19, 27, 32, 106, 124, 127, 133
  framework 7, 17, 27
  narrative 2
Nestorians 91, 147
new economic sociology 8, 132
Non-Muslims 24, 57, 102
North Africa 11, 92

Ömer Mansur of Libya 78
Ottoman
  bureaucracy 19, 26, 50, 60, 69, 102
  centralization 5, 56, 59, 60, 89
  history 10, 15–24, 26, 30, 33, 101
  Land Code 24, 59, 64, 78, 87, 88, 93, 134
  reforms 18, 30

Pagden, Anthony 1, 131
Palestine 4, 5, 13, 28, 39, 55, 57, 65, 67, 69, 73, 74, 110, 112–115, 124, 137, 148
Pamuk, Şevket 24, 132, 134, 137, 138, 141, 143, 145, 150
pan-Arabism 112, 114, 115
  pan-Arabist movement 112
pan-Islamism 29, 81, 103, 144
pan-Turkism 114
path-dependency 2–4, 7, 121, 122, 124, 127, 128, 130, 131
  path-making 4, 7
  reinforcing processes 3
  turning points 3, 4, 16, 22, 23, 26, 30, 68, 94, 124, 131
patrimonialism 5, 6, 55, 67–69, 131, 141
peasantry 24, 37, 46, 57, 85, 88, 89, 138
peasant studies 24
pilgrimage 85, 86
political history 32, 144, 146
port-city 4–6, 8, 22, 35, 38, 39, 41–46, 48–53, 104, 106–109, 120, 129, 138, 139
  press 5, 35, 52
  port-towns 39, 45, 48, 52, 109, 137, 139
  professionals 5, 45, 52, 103
post-colonial analysis 15, 30–32
protection rent 6, 10, 75, 86
Provincial Administration Law 78
provincial capitals 64, 72, 129
Public Debt Administration 23, 76

Index

Qing China (see China)
Quataert, Donald 24, 66, 133–137, 139, 142, 143

Rashid Rida 111
rational-choice theory 9
  principal–agent problems 9, 81, 125, 132
  monitoring costs 9, 81
  rebellion 9, 94–96, 98, 116, 146, 147, 152
Red Sea 87
Regie Company 24
regional paths 4, 34, 99, 101, 120, 121, 124, 126, 129
Reilly, James 59, 135, 136, 141, 142
Reinkowski, Maurus 76, 143
religious fees 10, 86
religious trust networks 5, 6, 120
resistance 1, 5, 22, 26, 49, 50, 56, 66, 76, 83, 84, 87, 90, 91, 93, 95, 97–99, 109, 114, 115, 118, 123, 135, 138, 140, 144, 145, 147, 149
Riyad 154
Russia 10, 18, 25, 76, 81, 102, 104, 118, 134, 152, 154

Safad 59, 141
salam contracts 64
Salonica 24, 37, 38, 42, 43, 48, 49, 104, 107, 108, 137–140, 148, 149
  Hamdi Bey of Salonica 43
  Tobacco Workers Union of Salonica 48
Salt 89, 154
Salzmann, Ariel 29, 135, 141, 153
Samsun 39, 48, 137, 139
Sana'a 86, 91, 129
Sarkal 87
Saud of Najd 83, 87, 91, 92, 120
Sayyid Talip 116
schooling 29, 74
Second Constitutional Period 18, 20, 30, 50, 78, 101, 126, 129

security 57, 64, 77, 78, 85, 89, 118, 144
sedentarization 57, 78, 86, 89, 138
Seferberlik 111
Selim III 17, 18, 102
şeyh 57, 82, 83, 89, 119, 147, 152
  Nehri Şeyhs 83
seyid 82, 89, 93
Shammar Tribe 86
Shukri Asali 110
Sivas 73, 130, 147, 149
smuggling 87, 98, 117
social darwinism 30
social history 22, 32
sovereignty 1, 22, 26, 75, 132
  deficit 132
  domestic 27, 132
  Ottoman 75
Stark, David 3, 132
state-building 3, 7, 28, 31, 75, 80, 84, 121, 123
state-formation 97
sub-contracting 66
Süleymaniye 86
Syria 4, 5, 13, 39, 55–57, 60, 64–67, 69, 73, 74, 110–112, 114, 118, 124, 125, 127, 140, 149, 153
  Northern Syria 24, 66
  Southern Syria 65, 82, 83, 84, 89, 90, 116, 119, 144

Tabak, Faruk 126, 132, 134, 142, 153
Tanzimat 16–18, 20, 29, 30, 42, 57, 69, 76, 81, 102, 133
tax 39, 50, 56, 63, 65, 78, 86, 87, 93, 115, 116, 127, 129, 139, 140, 144, 146, 153
  collection 58, 60, 63, 81, 85, 87, 93
  tax-farming 28, 29, 32, 58, 63, 88, 95, 98, 141
  agents 29, 36, 39, 46, 57, 137, 139, 151
textile 65–67, 89
Thelen, Kathleen 3, 131
Third-World 21, 22, 132

Thompson, Elizabeth 59, 141
Tilly, Charles 8, 33, 127, 132, 145, 146, 153, 154
Tokat 66
Toprak, Zafer 25, 133, 135
trade 5–7, 16, 22–24, 26, 35–39, 41, 46–50, 52, 57, 64, 65, 73, 85, 87, 89, 90, 98, 107, 108, 127, 131, 134, 137, 139, 140, 146
    export 36, 37, 39, 65, 87, 137
    free 5, 39, 50, 52, 64, 131
    import 24, 37
    long-distance 36, 57, 85, 136
    networks 22, 36, 37, 65, 126
    towns 24
transaction costs 90, 147
Transjordan 83, 84, 89, 90, 98, 106, 116, 135, 144, 145, 151, 153
Treaty of Da'an 98
Treaty of Sèvres 118
Tripoli 65, 109
Tujjar families 69
Tulip Era 20
Turkification 106, 110, 150
Turkish Revolution 25

urban Muslim bloc 5, 8, 45, 55, 60, 74, 97, 120, 123, 124, 148

vakıf 59, 60, 83, 142
Van 82, 87, 147, 148

Wahhabi Clans 85, 93, 147
West 1, 16–22, 25–27, 30, 33, 38, 42, 44, 57, 81, 94, 111, 135
    western impact 11, 17, 20
    westernization 16, 18–21, 25, 121, 137
Wong, Roy Bin 10, 73, 133, 135, 143
workers 22, 24, 25, 42, 48–50, 89, 107, 120, 143
world economy 2, 5, 15, 16, 21–26, 30, 32, 33, 35, 36, 38, 39, 45, 46, 50, 62, 66, 67, 102, 126, 138, 144
world history 10, 12
World War I 25, 98, 111, 119, 123, 139, 151
World War II 121
World-Systems Approach 8, 10, 15, 22, 23, 25, 26, 32, 134

Yemen 77, 78, 80, 83–87, 91–96, 116, 117, 124, 135, 145, 151
    Imam Yahya of Yemen 86, 91, 93, 98, 117
    Zaydi Imams of Yemen 83, 86
Young Arab Society (Fatat) 111
Young Ottomans 42
Young Turk Revolution 30, 99, 107, 126

za'im 108
Zionism 110, 148
Zor 78